The Baltimore
Book of the Dead

ALSO BY MARION WINIK

Highs in the Low Fifties
The Glen Rock Book of the Dead
Above Us Only Sky
Rules for the Unruly
The Lunch-Box Chronicles
First Comes Love
Telling
BoyCrazy
nonstop

The Baltimore
Book of the Dead

Marion Winik

COUNTERPOINT
BERKELEY, CALIFORNIA

For DDP, Baltimore friend through thick and thin

The Baltimore Book of the Dead

Copyright © 2018 by Marion Winik
First hardcover edition: 2018

Library of Congress Cataloging-in-Publication Data
Names: Winik, Marion, author.
Title: The Baltimore book of the dead / Marion Winik.
Description: Berkeley, California : Counterpoint, [2018] |
Includes bibliographical references.
Identifiers: LCCN 2018012453 | ISBN 9781640091214
Subjects: LCSH: Winik, Marion—Anecdotes. |
Death—Anecdotes. | Curiosities and wonders. |
Baltimore (Md.)—Biography.
Classification: LCC CT275.W584626 A2 2018 |
DDC 975.2/6—dc23
LC record available at https://lccn.loc.gov/2018012453

Jacket designed by Jenny Carrow

COUNTERPOINT
2560 Ninth Street, Suite 318
Berkeley, CA 94710
www.counterpointpress.com

Printed in Canada
Distributed by Publishers Group West

1 3 5 7 9 10 8 6 4 2

People do not pass away.
They die
and then they stay.

—NAOMI SHIHAB NYE, *Voices in the Air*

Contents

Introduction

DURING THE SPRING OF 2007, in the dark days
toward the end of our marriage, my second husband
and I managed to get ourselves invited to a small
house party on the South Coast of Jamaica, held over
the weekend of the Calabash Festival, a major annual
literary event with writers from all over the Carib-
bean and the world. I had just begun writing *The Glen
Rock Book of the Dead*, the predecessor to this volume.

The first morning, all the guests went up the road to
Jake's, the resort where the festival is held, in our hosts'
van. We heard readings, paged through books on sale,
sipped frozen drinks. My husband and I sipped many
of them. The group went home for lunch, planning
to return in the afternoon, but storm clouds massed
and broke and no one wanted to go back in the pouring rain.

Our friends were expecting another visitor for
drinks that evening. This man turned out to be a writer
for the island's main newspaper and also a native of

the fishing village where the house was located. He spoke passionately about Jamaica's history and politics. He told us about his father and his uncles and cousins, many of them claimed by the greedy sea. One story after another poured out of him, stories of people dying in boats, in hurricanes, on cliffs, people dying even at other people's funerals.

I asked if he would write about them, and he said he planned to, told me how it would begin with him standing on the beach with his aunt Lucy when he was very young, trying to understand the look on her face as she watched the ocean.

After he left, we sat down to dinner: our hosts, four other friends of theirs, my husband, now definitively in the bag, and me. The rain hammered on the roof as the local women who worked for them brought dishes of callaloo and jerk meats.

Since we were skipping the evening program at the festival, I suggested that after dinner I could fill in with a reading from the collection I was working on. The pieces were very new and I hadn't had the opportunity to get people's reactions. I was eager to do so. I wished that the journalist had still been there, but the other guests seemed interested enough.

The first one I read was about my father; the second was called "The Realtor," about the spunky Texas woman who had sold my house years back. The short piece had several scenes, one in Venice, one in her backyard, one in her bedroom when she was dying of cancer. I had barely finished it when one of the women at the table blurted emotionally, Please, I'm on vacation. I don't want to hear this depressing stuff. She jumped up with her hand over her mouth and fled to her room.

I wanted to go to her, but my hostess thought I should not. Well, then, I said, why don't I just continue. My hostess didn't think much of that idea, either. At this point, she was well on her way to regretting having invited us, and we would both give her further reasons to do so for the remainder of the weekend, the final mistake being leaving too small a tip for the staff, which I still feel bad about.

I reluctantly put aside my laptop. A debate ensued among the remaining guests about just how depressing the pieces really were, and whether the topic of death had any proper place at the dinner table.

I suggested that, at least from my perspective, our lives are so full of dead people that any sane way of living involves constant remembrance. My days and my thoughts are shaped almost as much by people who are no longer here as those who are. That to cast this remembrance as depressing is to deprive ourselves of our history, our context, and even one of our pleasures, if a bittersweet one. Meeting the journalist earlier in the evening had been a more meaningful experience because he'd told us about his father and uncles.

Death is the subtext of life, there is no way around it. It is the foundation of life's meaning and value. It is the ultimate game-changer, the shift in perspective that puts everything in its place, yet it is a part of our story we know little about and have little control over.

So at the very least, it's interesting.

On the other hand, as far as death at the dinner table goes, some respectful space must be made for grief. Grief is socially awkward, if not all-out anti-social, difficult to accommodate even in one-on-one conversations. Even now, when I mention that I was widowed in my first marriage, or that my first baby was stillborn, I see people's faces fall, and I rush to explain that it was a long, long time ago and it was very sad but I am fine now. I really am. But I am also trying to spare them the awkwardness of having to come up with some appropriate, or more likely inappropriate, response, perhaps making some well-intentioned but doomed attempt to help me get over it, possibly by implying that it was God's will.

Which brings me back to the time when I was not fine, after those deaths and others, as well, and there I find part of my motivation for writing these books, for dwelling so long in the graveyard, for finding a way to talk about it.

In times of intense grief, I have tried all the usual methods of escape—distraction, compensation, intoxication; therapies and treatments and antidotes for body and soul. I once had a massage from a woman named Chaka that unleashed a hurricane of tears. Ultimately, instead of attempting to flee from the pain of loss, I decided to spend time with it, to linger, to let these thoughts and feelings bloom inside me into something else.

Why do we build memorials, decorate gravesites, set up shrines, stitch an AIDS quilt, paint three murals for Freddie Gray; what are these ghostly white bicycles woven with flowers on Charles and Roland avenues? These are places to put our grief, places outside ourselves. And when you make a memorial object with your own hands, some of the anguish dissolves into what you are making. You are returned from the world of the dead to the world of the living.

For example, that ex-husband of mine never tired of hearing the heartbreaking song "Sweet Old World" by Lucinda Williams. Addressed to Williams's boyfriend who died of an overdose, the song was for him a way of connecting with his feelings about another loss—his younger brother, dead of similar causes when he was barely thirty. *See what you lost when you left this world, this sweet old world . . .*

Part of the beauty of the song, like so many other songs of mourning, is that people hear and feel in it a reflection of their own grief. When my fatherless sons were teenagers, they fell in love with songs by Blink-182 and OPM about people who died too young. It takes away some of the brutal loneliness of bereavement to hear those lyrics, or to read that story, to see the monument someone else has made by hand. To join a chain of remembering. It does not

make us any sadder to consume these morbid enter-
tainments; it may even ease our hearts.

The novelist Lewis Nordan, remembered later
in these pages, has a beautiful short story called
"Tombstone" about a man whose son committed suicide fourteen years earlier. The man comes
across a photograph of folk-art tombstones from
the South. They are blocks of poured concrete, with
wings and heads projecting from the base, the wings
washed white and the faces painted simply to rep-
resent the lost people. Driven to make one of these
for his son, the narrator says, *A joy I had not felt for
fourteen years swam into my heart as I fashioned Robin's sweet closed eyes, as I remembered having seen them
in sleep, and a trace of his pickerel smile.*

The "pickerel smile" is a reference to another literary memorial, Theodore Roethke's "Elegy for Jane,
My Student Thrown by a Horse." *I remember the neck-
curls, limp and damp as tendrils / And her quick look, a
sidelong pickerel smile . . .*

A pickerel, by the way, is a young pike. Apparently
famous for their smiles.

After that trip to Jamaica, 2007 went straight down-
hill. The marriage was almost over, and in September my mother was diagnosed with lung cancer. Every
time I went to visit her, we would talk about different
people I wanted to include in the book; there was so

much I didn't know. Meanwhile, it started to be obvious that she could soon become one of its characters. Hell, no, I thought, quickly completing and turning in the manuscript so she would not be in it, as if this would have mystical power to keep her alive.

Ten years later, this second book begins with her, adding people who died between 2008 and 2017, and a few others. Some of them I loved, some of them I barely knew, some I only worshipped from afar, but all of their deaths I considered a subtraction from my world. I have made every attempt to be accurate about the details of their lives, yet as in the previous volume I have omitted their names, since they had no chance to correct any errors, or even agree to be in this book.

I moved from rural Pennsylvania—Glen Rock—to Baltimore in February of 2009. So like its predecessor, this book is named for the place I wrote it, rather than the stories it includes. But you can't call a book *The Baltimore Book of the Dead* without creating certain expectations.

This city has a vexed and unnaturally intimate relationship with death. In Bodymore, Murderland, as the poets call it, people will sometimes refer to their relative who was a homicide victim as "Number 146," meaning he was the 146th of the people murdered this year. Last year, according to the *Baltimore Sun*, the number got to 343. Back before these official counts were so widely publicized, I taught a student in the MFA program at the University of

Baltimore, a young black man who grew up here. He had filled a shoebox with obituaries of friends and family by the time he was in high school. You'll meet his brother in a little while.

Well before the death of Freddie Gray and the uprising that followed, people who came to visit me would ask if it is very frightening and dangerous to live in Baltimore. They wondered if they would be safe. Well, of course, they had seen *The Wire*. Has any other television show so shaped the reputation of a city?

I would explain that the Baltimore they were visiting is a narrow strip of relative privilege and safety, a column of nice neighborhoods through which the more privileged citizens oscillate, dropping our kids at school, heading to our offices at Hopkins or MICA, drinking microbrews in converted mill buildings, tooling down to the Inner Harbor in hybrid cars to openings at the Visionary Art Museum.

To the left and right of this spinal cord of gentrification is another Baltimore, the stubbled flanks of the city: crumbling projects, blocks and blocks of boarded-up row homes, crowded bus stops, street-corner car washes, churches, hairdressers, liquor stores, and chicken shacks. There are people who live two miles from the glitzy Inner Harbor who have never seen it, and we won't be visiting their neighborhoods, either, unless the GPS screws up. It is a loss for all of us.

During the chaos of May 2015, friends all over the country checked in to make sure I was all right. I'm watching it on TV, I told them, just like you are. The day our city schools were closed, a few of us moms organized a little peace march with the kids in our neighborhood, parading down the main avenue with brown-paper signs, banging on pots and chanting slogans. Public life has only gotten more alarming and alienating since then, and Baltimore remains two cities, not one. No matter what happens, there will always be as many books of the dead as there are people remembering.

MARION WINIK
Baltimore, Maryland
March 2018

The Baltimore
Book of the Dead

The Alpha

ANYONE WHO WAS AT Camp Nawita in the late 1930s
can tell you, she was queen of the baseball diamond.
The tennis court, the hockey field, the horseshoe pitch,
and the lake. Too bad she beat Title IX by forty years.
It wasn't exactly the heyday of female business majors,
either, nor women in the workplace, and for a really bad
idea, try sending a young woman on a business trip by
herself, wedding ring or no. Enough already. She got
pregnant, moved to the Shore, took up golf and gin.
She won her first club championship in 1966, just as I
began my poetry career. I raced into the dining room
where she was drinking her martini, ode in hand. *She
had a bad lie in the weeds of sixteen / Ere she lofted and
landed her ball on the green.* Now I haven't set eyes on
that place in ten years, and when they say everything is
different, I believe them.

Everyone's mother is mythological: her body the ori-
gin of existence and consciousness, her house the

pimped-out crib of Zeus, her mistakes the cause of everything. Holy her rosebushes, holy her blackjack system, her London broil holy. My mother, the godhead of 7 Dwight Drive, rose daily from her bed to quaff her Tropicana orange juice and to slay the *New York Times* crossword puzzle. She survived a difficult childhood, my father's high jinks, two heart attacks, non-Hodgkin's lymphoma, surgery for diverticulosis, and the many poor decisions and inappropriate outfits of her daughters. She certainly did not believe a clot in her lung could bring her down, that smoking for sixty-five years would actually cause lung cancer, or that lung cancer was definitely fatal. The last thing she did before she took to her bed was win a golf tournament. Clearly the subprime crisis, the market crash, Hurricane Sandy, and even Donald Trump were biding their time until she was out of the way.

And then she was. Imagine Persephone coming up from hell and Demeter not there. Strange cars in the driveway, the rosebushes skeletons. You stand there at first, uncomprehending, your poem in your hand. Then you go somewhere, call it home. Call it spring.

The Perfect Couple

died 1991, 2011

IT IS 1956 AT the beach club, the whole crew lined up on lounges like glamorous crayons. She's the one with the legs, the baby, just back from boring old freshman year. Have you two met? someone asks, and she looks up from her Bain de Soleil. Why, that's the sweetest smile she's ever seen. Poof, there goes college.

In 1965, she was the prettiest mom at my seventh birthday party, with her long, swinging hair and white patent leather belt, her third little bundle in the stroller. She wanted more but the doctor said no. Too many miscarriages, and this guy came two months early and almost didn't make it. Then there's the problem the doctor doesn't know about.

Having been in a marriage something like hers decades later, I suspect she knew the truth about her husband early on—but as long as she could pretend, she absolutely did. They were the best-looking couple in town, and so much fun. And she had her three darlings; how lonely could she be? The kids were in their teens when she finally cracked. It was the third night of Hanukkah, all of them standing around the menorah wide-eyed as he headed for the door. Go, go, she screamed into the street. Just go.

There was no shortage of suitors for both of them, no shortage of busybodies and bigots, either. It was almost a relief when he moved to an apartment in the city. In some ways, he had picked the best of all times to come out, the Manhattan of the seventies and eighties, the Limelight, the Boy Bar, Studio 54. And also the worst of times: as the eighties ended, he got a sore on his foot that wouldn't heal. She came as soon as he told her and stayed through the end, grumbling boyfriends on both sides notwithstanding.

After that, it just kept getting harder with cameras and mirrors: once allies, now bullies to be avoided. You don't want to care so much, but how do you stop? Mom, the kids would scold when she'd try to slip out of a photo or bury her face in the nearest grandchild. Don't be silly, you look fine. She did adore them all, but when Mr. Lung Cancer knocked on the door, she was ready. Give me a just a minute, dear. I'll be right down.

The Fourth

A CARD TABLE WITH a felted cloth, two brand-new, slippery decks, a long, skinny score pad divided into mysterious quadrants. Folding tables set catty-corner for the ashtrays and glasses, a dish of flavored almonds, a crystal bowl of shiny chocolate balls. These come from the candy store on Route 35 and are only for bridge, which is why they're called bridge mix. North and South put their kids to bed; East and West ring the doorbell. Drinks are poured. The door to the kitchen is closed. Game on.

The fact that my parents' best friends were less ferocious than they were doesn't mean they couldn't beat them. Two diamonds. Three hearts. Three no trump. Pass. Pass. Pass. Over the whole twenty-year rivalry, which ended only with my father's early death, I bet they were even. When the game was at their house, I might be taken along: they had a brown-and-white dog named Clementine and a cute son my age. We had a very serious romance when we were eleven.

West was tall, with curly hair, kind eyes, and rectangular wire-rimmed glasses on his excellent nose. He was president of the JCC, had two businesses in Asbury: a carpet store and the U-pedal boats at the boardwalk. I worked at the boats one summer when I was a teenager, then later caused trouble by writing in my first book about how we workers embezzled money to buy beer. I did a lot of stupid things like this in the early days of my writing. That whole first book was what old Jews call a shonda for the goyim.

Poor East: West could not play cards, or drive, or even answer the phone in the very long confusion that was the end of his life, through which East stood unflinchingly by him. The last time I saw him we had to explain who I was. Hy and Jane's daughter. You remember. The one who stole money from the boats.

The Cat with Nine Lives
died 2016

DISEASES DIDN'T KILL HIM (polio, leukemia, von Willebrand's), history left him standing (World War II, Korea, market crash of '87), his marriages proved nonlethal, and one escape was sheer James Bond: a collision between a commuter seaplane and a police helicopter over Brooklyn that killed everyone involved except him and a woman whose life he saved. Just after the plane hit the water, he forced open the emergency exit and pulled her out, then tried to get back into the rapidly sinking plane. The other passenger was his buddy, a fellow stockbroker with kids the same age— but the current tore the door out of his hands, just as it would in his nightmares for years to come. How did he get to shore with a broken back, a split-open head, and an unconscious woman? the reporters asked. We were lucky, he told them. Just lucky.

This modest hero was my mother's favorite cousin— an old-school gentleman who loved a good joke and a good cigar. He had a seat on the stock exchange for forty years. He called his own mother every morning. His boys were the center of his universe, and they worshipped him in return. He never raised his voice at home, and the first time his older son heard him curse in anger he was seventeen years old: he had gone to work with his father on the trading floor. His ninth life lasted seven years, the long goodbye of losses and forgetting. This is when Sweetums, which is what my father used to call his wife, not to her face, and not because she was, became a hero, too. He would have hated being such a burden, but of course he barely knew about it. The only consolations of Alzheimer's, and they are small indeed, is that it doesn't hurt much, and that once the full nightmare is under way, you are long gone.

The Man Who Could Take Off His Thumb

died 2009

THROUGH THE SIXTIES AND seventies, my father had various businesses, among them a motel, a discotheque, and a small chain of tennis facilities grandly dubbed National Sports Corporation. He co-owned National Sports with his uncle, who was so much younger than my grandfather that he and my dad had grown up as peers.

From our youngest years, my sister and I were in the employ of National Sports, one of us reading numbers off receipts as the other totaled them using a furiously grinding adding machine. We were often taken along when my father went after-hours to the indoor club near our house. Inside the corrugated metal walls that enclosed the three courts hung a second wall of thick green vinyl, creating a darkened corridor around the perimeter of the immense space, full of stray tennis balls. If that were not paradise enough, there was also a sauna.

One of my parents' friends claimed he could turn you into a puppy, another played a game with stair steps and pennies, and my uncle had a trick where he pretended to take off his thumb. He lived in Rye, New York, and he was married to a woman whom my father referred to as Piano Legs, though whether this was a compliment or an insult, I don't know. Piano Legs died in the 1970s, and my uncle remarried a friend of hers, a formidable woman who worked for the cause of Israel and that of Soviet dissidents, who knew David Ben-Gurion, Golda Meir, and Moshe Dayan. She and my uncle had quite a run, living at the tennis camp in the summers and in winters, traveling the world: Easter Island, Alaska, climbing in the Himalayas, floating down the Amazon.

At seventy-three, my uncle began to have symptoms of Alzheimer's, and his wife kept a diary of her experiences for the next ten years. She self-published a book about it, and yesterday a copy arrived from Amazon. In it I found pictures of my uncle doing his thumb trick for little kids in Brazil and Moscow. What luck he had, to marry this woman, whose obituary only recently appeared in the *Palm Beach Post*. *Our life together has had its share of pain,* she wrote on the last page of her book, *but its share of joy as well. Perhaps the greatest reward in this kind of situation is the knowledge that you have not failed the person you love.*

The Classmate

PROBABLY BECAUSE SHE LIVED in our hometown all her life, I recognize the names in her guest book at Legacy.com. Old classmates have posted reminiscences about driving into school together, about working side by side at the Foodtown. A boy who'd known her since kindergarten tells how they laughed to find themselves in class together yet again at the local college. Many write of her laugh: a throaty chuckle you didn't expect from that skinny reed of a girl.

She had a long, shallowly sculpted Eastern European face, light eyes and long blond hair, a very Slavic series of consonants in her last name. Whether for her complexion or her disposition or both, she was always called Peaches, even in school. Her older brothers were famous in our town for their basketball feats; she herself made girls' varsity our freshman year. After her father left, her mom raised seven kids alone, working full-time. My classmate was the oldest daughter, mother #2. When girls who have that childhood don't start families later on, it makes a certain sense. They've done it already.

She worked most of her life on displays for department stores, a job she loved: a tall, stylish woman, hair cropped, often amused. She never hid what she really thought; she always had that laugh. She was just fifty-two the day she went home from work early on Friday and was dead by Sunday, a mystery that's really never been solved. Liver failure, Tylenol, that's what we heard. There were hundreds of people at the viewing, many of them old classmates, shocked and sad. We had thought we were still young.

Two First Cousins

died 2008, 2012

My cousin and I are together in the playpen. We wear thick white diapers and rubber pants that leave red circles on our chunky thighs. The game is pull yourself up on the nylon mesh walls and scoot around the edge of the pen. Already my cousin is a gentleman; he lets me go first. Our mommies are pregnant again, standing at the counter in their tented maternity blouses, a cigarette burning in the ashtray. They are stuffing celery sticks with a mixture of cream cheese, Roquefort, and Worcestershire, a recipe left by their own mother before she ran off and died young of a heart attack.

Ten years later. In the half-finished upstairs room on Dwight Drive, my little sister and I are making my cousin show us his penis. We did the same thing the other day to a boy down the street; apparently we are taking inventory. My cousin remains gallant, if red in the face: if we really must see it he will show us. His

own little sister watches in awe, half admiring our ter-
ribleness, half bristling at her brother's subjugation.

The big brother did everything right. Worked in his
father's paint store, did pull-ups and push-ups every
morning, brought bagels to his parents' house on
weekends. His little sister did not follow his example. She meant no harm and I don't believe she hurt
a soul, but she never escaped the fallout of some early
bad decisions involving a glass pipe.

Hearts are a problem in our family: A few weeks after
his fiftieth birthday party, at his peak and prime, my
cousin went into the bathroom one morning and did
not come out. His sister continued paying for her
mistakes for another four years. Possessions disappeared, blood sugar spiked, toes were amputated. The
night her little dog disappeared, it almost killed her,
then all the other stuff actually did.

Since we have to live as if our choices matter, perhaps
we should not dwell on the story of my two first cousins. Unless you can think of something else it can possibly mean.

Their Mother

TODAY I DROVE TO Delaware to see my aunt buried between the tombstones of her two children. It was a Jewish funeral, so the mourners passed a shovel among them to throw dirt on the coffin. My uncle seemed to have shrunk to the size of a large doll.

In my childhood, we drove to Delaware every Thanksgiving. It was six hours round trip and my father was a total ass about it, but that was just his way. The best thing was my aunt's stuffed artichokes, packed with lemony, garlicky breadcrumbs. For years I thought stuffed artichokes were like cranberry sauce or sweet potatoes with marshmallows, a special food eaten only on Thanksgiving. She also introduced us to the joy of the miniature dachshund, the official dog breed of our family to this day.

When my aunt was eight years old and my mother sixteen, their mother ran off with another man, leaving them in the care of their father, a terrible tyrant. Even as it dumped on my mother a life-changing overabundance of responsibility, this turn of events so traumatized my aunt that she suffered a period of hysterical paralysis. (I heard this so often as a child that I recite it here with confidence, though I have never heard this condition mentioned in any other context.) From that time on, my aunt was well aware that the universe was against her. What god makes a mother bury both of her children? Still, she had to get through the days, so she doted on my uncle and found joy where she could. Shopping. Lunch. Studies have been conducted to prove that smiling, even if you don't feel like smiling, will actually make you happier. My aunt could have told them that. I think she could have told them exactly how much.

In later years, I never saw her without a jigsaw puzzle spread out on her dining room table. This was the legacy of the terrible tyrant, who had raised his daughters with strict rules about puzzle procedure. First you find the edges and put them together. Then you sort the other pieces by color. You never pick up a piece unless you already know where it goes. There is a piece for every spot, and if there isn't, check under the table. There's no luck about it. Keep going, and you will receive one of life's few predictable satisfactions, the joy of putting in the last piece.

The Social Worker

MY MOTHER HAD FEW close friends who weren't serious about golf. Also rare among her cronies were large families, professional careers, and divorces, at least in the early part of my childhood. Yet one of her dearest confidantes was a pert brunette with a great figure who had five kids, an ex-husband, a master's degree in social work, and a full-time job in the field. While this woman thought it was funny that someone as smart as my mother would devote her life to playing games, my mother could not believe that anyone had actually set out to have so many children. Well, the last two were twins. Twins! A prospect almost as petrifying to Jane Winik as stepchildren.

The social worker always made me feel I was one of her favorites, stopping to visit whenever I was home from college. My mother did the same over there. As we kids grew up, we followed the story of each other's family like a long-running TV series. Her oldest boy got into Dartmouth, my mother would report. His brother had moved to the West Coast with some guys from high school. The cheerleader went into finance, the dancer had a show in the city, the other twin became very Jewish and moved to Israel. Five kids, just like her mother. Oy!

Among the many fascinating details of this soap opera, there is a plot line that remains veiled in mystery. Why did the oldest daughter see "a silver man in a silver car," revealed to be my dad, in front of their house one Tuesday afternoon? What went on at that discotheque of his, which her mother loved and my mother found utterly ridiculous? Was it all just a rumor, or were the seventies as Bob and Carol and Ted and Alice as people imagine? All we know is that they remained friends for the rest of their lives.

In her last years, the social worker moved to California to be near her oldest daughter and her grandchildren. At a certain point, she forgot she had retired and thought she was seeing patients at the facility where she herself was being treated. I'm not ready for this appointment, she would suddenly cry. Her daughter would calm her by explaining that the client had rescheduled.

Oh, good, said her mother. That will give me time.

The Mensch

WHEN IT CAME TIME to describe her father's achievements in his obituary, my oldest friend wrote this: *He spent much of his life in New Jersey, providing for his family and relaxing at local beaches.* Indeed. Her handsome, dark-eyed father was one of the most solicitous and generous people I have ever met. You must be thirsty; let me get you a glass of water. Wine? No? How about a snack? After my parents were gone and the house on Dwight Drive sold, I could show up down the street and get a hero's welcome. Then we'd hit the beach in Asbury, and he would take the kids swimming so we lazy mamas could lounge around and read.

Most of his life he was a car dealer, selling British Leyland imports, and despite my friend's prescient badgering about the environmental cost of automobiles, her first car was a 1972 baby blue MGB Midget that shut her mouth. Then, the summer we were eighteen, he won a red Triumph convertible in a sales contest and arranged for us to pick it up at the factory in England. Somewhere south of Paris we rolled the car into a ditch in the process of pulling over for the cyclists of the Tour de France. It seemed just fine when it was dragged out by a tractor, but the next day as we left, weeds tangled in the undercarriage caught fire. But even then, it got us all the way down to Nice, up through the Alps, into Berlin, and back to Calais. The only time I can remember her father being angry was upon that car's return to the United States.

When you're eighty, a lot of things are long ago: tough decisions, hard times, regrets, all far away now. Watching him in his garden, or with our little girls in the shallow water, you could get the idea he'd been waiting all his life just for this. To be a deeply tanned, slightly stooped old Jewish man, standing at the water's edge in turquoise trunks and a white terry-cloth bucket hat. Surely if he'd been given the chance, he'd be standing there still.

The Thin White Duke

died 2016

THERE ARE TWO KINDS of rock star: the kind you want to sleep with, and the kind you want to be—though in most cases either would be fine. A poet friend told me that the high point of her life was when she appeared as Ziggy Stardust at a twenty-fifth-anniversary celebration of the album at Yale. (A second-generation fan, she was not even born when we were listening to *Hunky Dory* on endless loop in 1971.) She cut off her hair, dyed it red, wore a jumpsuit and silver platform boots. She sang every song on the album. Though this was the entire history of her career as a vocalist, she was so carried off by euphoria that she married the drummer.

In my early adolescence, I had a kind of mild gender dysphoria, though I have only learned that term relatively recently. Nagged by the feeling that things would be working out better for me if I'd been born a boy, one summer at camp I told people my name was Mike. It wasn't that I was attracted to girls. In fact, the teenage me was more interested in gay men than gay women, making continual heroic efforts to be admitted to El Moroccan Room, a drag club in Asbury Park. Gender, sexuality, art, music, rebellion: all of this made more sense because of him. He gave us a bigger space to decide who to be.

Of his many performance personae—Ziggy Stardust, Major Tom, Aladdin Sane, Screaming Lord Byron, The Goblin King—The Thin White Duke was definitely the worst idea. A stylish blond neo-romantic hero, the Aryan Duke caused a hullabaloo by saying things like Hitler was the first rock star. Bowie later explained that he was doing so much cocaine at this time that he had no memory of even recording the album *Station to Station* (one of my favorites, his haunting, shaky cover of "Wild Is the Wind," comes from this period). He ended it by moving away from Los Angeles. Luckily, what usually happens to rock stars when drugs get the better of them happened only to The Thin White Duke, not his creator. David Bowie lived another forty years, even completing an afterword to his body of work in "Lazarus." He was leaving his cell phone down here, he said, to be free.

The Camp Director

died 2017

My sister and I hated sleepaway camp, which didn't get us out of going, but did get us sent to a different place every year. As far as I could see, the lanyards, the archery, the outhouses were the same everywhere. Then I came upon this in the summer camp ads in the *New York Times*: *Greenfields. A "happening" for the youngster who desires to explore creative interests.*

The "happening" was in a fairy-tale forest with a deep quarry pool outside Woodstock, New York. Its director was a public school teacher who bought a small, dilapidated Catskills resort from his grandmother, then turned the place into a summer camp for kids aged twelve to sixteen. When we pulled into the driveway in 1972 in my mother's emerald green sedan, he bounded out to meet us in some sort of flowing robe, tall and hearty, with a head of curls and an exuberant beard. His charisma and confidence were such that he and my buttoned-up mother quickly developed an unlikely mutual respect.

What a camp! No songs, no traditions, real flush toilets! We made things out of stained glass and copper enamel, swam in the spillway of the Ashokan Reservoir, hiked Slide Mountain. The whole camp saw the Dead and the Allman Brothers at Watkins Glen. Boone's Farm apple wine abuse, extreme teen melodrama, and spoiled brats were handled by the camp director with tough love and good humor. Cooking and cleaning were "community service" and, like that hellacious hike, you were not getting out of it.

When I peeked in forty years later, he'd become a potter and the bunks had become a craft gallery. His curls had grayed and his face had weathered but his sarong-wrapped, leonine presence had lost none of its roar. Then one day his second wife found him crumpled among the silver bracelets and stained glass windows. He left us a few days later, having demonstrated conclusively that real men wear caftans and that it's not just okay but necessary and gorgeous to be who you are.

My Advisor

died 2017

I LEFT HIGH SCHOOL with a vow never to study history again; only earth science had a looser grip on my imagination. But when I got to college, I chose my classes by asking around for the names of the rock star professors. The Mick Jagger of them all was the Russian History guy. The class he was teaching in the fall of 1978, "Russia before 1800," was limited to upperclassmen. But since doing things I wasn't allowed to do was my most passionate avocation, I went to his office to make my case.

The professor was a tall, lanky fellow with dark hair combed straight back from his high forehead and black horn-rimmed glasses, a kind of academic Clark Kent, in whose hands the epic saga of Russia was addictive, tragic, hilarious. For years I kept a pile of spiral notebooks filled with notes from his classes, sometimes copied from the board in an imitation of his eccentric, baroque handwriting, which somehow made English look like Cyrillic. False Dimitri, Michael Bakunin, Nizhny Novgorod. I was madly in. love with him, which I expressed by declaring a history major. We majors got to go over to his house and listen to jazz or watch the Red Sox. I was generally not a very good babysitter but for his kids I tried.

In later years, eager to show off this great person in my life—My Advisor, as I always referred to him—I brought friends and family to his house for an audience. By the last time I came through town, he had been struggling with Parkinson's for a decade. Unbelievably, he'd had to give up reading and writing; now his canvases leaned against the walls, abstract, Marsden Hartley–type paintings that had the feeling of jazz. After his memorial in Providence, filled with more illustrious and closer disciples than I, his wife and kids took me home with them rather than let me wander drunkenly into the night looking for my hotel. A glass of milk in the downstairs kitchen for the perennial crushed-out student, the very last one

The Golden Boy

ONE OF THE PEOPLE I idolized at college was a genius boy from Westchester with a motorcycle and well-stocked quiver of left-wing ideas. When I showed up in the fall of '75, he was on his way out west to attain biodegradable nirvana. One of his glamorous qualities was his charismatic older brother, who had arrived in Providence a few years ahead of us. This guy had ruled his prep school in Princeton and had taken over here, as well. He was already launched on what looked like a career in Rhode Island politics, while also managing a big local band and finishing his degree. This was a time when there was a lot of cocaine everywhere, including Wall Street and Hollywood, and his connections in that regard only added to his sparkle.

Then he crashed into the wall of a very serious bust that even their well-connected family could not completely fix, though the Golden Boy did no jail time. He never graduated, either. Instead he tumbled into a far-from-golden cycle: bailout, rehab, job placement, recovery, then just a little, why not. His little brother watched from a distance as his parents buckled under. He kept a list of beautiful, wrecked cars: GTO, Corolla, Tempest, Mustang, Fiat.

The last time he saw his brother, both were in their mid-fifties. By now my friend was a city planner, a proud father, a golden man, stopping in Florida on his way back from a tour of Cuba. He found an ancient-looking wreck with a rotating cycle of slurred, self-aggrandizing stories, nonetheless still able to rob you while telling you how much he loved you.

Some years later, he received a few boxes of personal effects gathered from the room where the Golden Boy had taken his last breath. A file of their mother's recipes, a vast collection of AA and NA paraphernalia, a framed story about him from a local magazine. And a scrapbook containing old black-and-white photographs of two little men, mugging for the camera in their overcoats, their suits and ties, the big one with his arm wrapped protectively around his smaller brother. As moved as my friend was, he found he could not remember those times at all.

The Warrior Poetess

WHEN I MOVED TO Texas in 1976, there was a rollicking poetry rodeo in full swing, featuring lyrical blowhards, Spanish-speaking divas, a taxi driver Kerouac, a deaf detective, grizzled drunkards, delicate Houstonians, and, moving regally among them, a somewhat terrifying queen: a soft-voiced, full-bodied woman with a cheerleader's smile and straight blond hair to her waist, a feminist, a pacifist, an activist, a relentless crusader, with a raised eyebrow that could hit every note from amused dubiety to all-out disgust.

I—an eighteen-year-old enfant terrible wearing a bustier or an ice-hockey uniform to read poems about my ill-advised liaisons—registered somewhere between the two. So we weren't close, and then I went away, and several decades later, I heard she had died. *A brief struggle with cancer,* said the obituary; though sixty-five is too young, perhaps brief is not so bad.

In the meantime, the press she started in 1975 had released 350 titles and she herself nineteen collections of verse, winning three Austin Book Awards, one Violet Crown Award, and the 1990 prize for Texas Woman of the Year. She founded festivals and conferences and workshops and mentored countless young writers, but as was suggested in the resolution of the eighty-second Texas Legislature that honored her life, she was known as much for swimming as for any of these things.

She swam every day year-round in the icy emerald waters of Barton Springs, where a single lap is a full half mile, where the pool, the birds, the cliffs, and the trees surrounding them were threatened by development, then aggressively assailed from every side, and she served on the committee and spoke at the meeting and recited poems at the city council to denounce this, *the men in black suits with their evil plans and pronouncements, their beards diplomas with no courses in literature or ethics, philosophy or art. Onetwothree breathe. Onetwothree—breathe.*

That is from her piece in the 1993 anthology *Barton Springs Eternal*, ed. Turk Pipkin, where we will always be together, her quietly furious and me half dressed. Poetry heaven.

The Jewish Floridian

died 2011

ALWAYS READY TO GET the party started, my first
husband and I took a trip to Miami right before our
wedding. We stayed with my oldest friend, who was
herself staying with her grandmother in her condo-
minium complex, where the newspaper slipped under
the door was the *Jewish Floridian*. My friend's elegant grandma was happy to have us, though she sent
us to dinner with her credit card rather than appear
with us in public. My hairdresser fiancé was sporting
platinum-blond hair extensions wrapped around his
head with rags, and I was running around in a blue
negligee and peignoir I had received as a shower gift.

If we had any sense, we would have listened to her
fashion advice. In the thirties, my friend's grandmother had started a dress shop on the front steps of
her mother's house on Ocean Parkway in Brooklyn,
an outgrowth of a lingerie business she and her sisters

had run after the war. Once the front steps got so busy the neighbors complained, she opened a real store on Neptune Avenue. Exclusive but not expensive, it was particularly beloved by wealthy Syrian Jews, who were moving to Brooklyn in droves as their homeland became increasingly anti-Semitic.

Who knows what would have happened career-wise if her heart hadn't been broken one day in 1951 when one of her two daughters was killed in a car crash. This darkness changed the story in ways nobody wants to remember anymore. My best friend was named after the aunt she never knew and was raised to select her clothes with passion and individuality. In the twenty-first century, she brought up her own daughter the same way. And so the one hundredth birthday of the Jewish Floridian was celebrated by four generations of beautiful women in beautiful clothes, and me in my blue jeans, bearing a homemade challah.

The last time I saw the Jewish Floridian, she was no longer in Florida but in an assisted living center by the Jersey Shore. It was a perfectly nice place, as these places go, though everyone who lives there just wants to know why can't they go home. Perhaps the answer was a sign in the lobby that looked like a ransom note, with cutout words collaged together. Today is Monday, August 10, 2009. The Season is SUMMER. The

Weather is HOT and HUMID, and The Next Holiday is LABOR DAY.

This may be everything about extreme old age I need to know.

The Brother-in-Law

IT STARTS WITH GIN and Wink in Tupperware tumblers on the dock of Lake Wallenpaupack in the Poconos, where I had come with the love of my life to meet his family. His younger brother was carrying the drinks from the house on a tray. A more compact, sturdy version of my willowy beau, he was by far the most hospitable person in the family. A wide smile on his face, goofy jokes, considerate ways. A Metallica T-shirt. A joint in his pocket for later. Hair thinning a little already, at twenty-four. I felt like I could have gone to high school with him, gotten high together during study hall. Fun-loving, super-bad white kids from the seventies, that's what we were.

Not long after we got married, my new brother-in-law got married, too—a hardworking, blue-eyed local girl with three young sons, close together in age, whom I always thought of as Huey, Dewey, and Louie. Helping her raise those boys was the best thing he ever did.

Never missed a ball game, a road trip to the beach, a night of fireworks on the lake. Having grown up himself with a nasty, violent dad and a gentle stepfather, he was nothing but kind to those boys, knew enough to leave the discipline to their mom.

Huey, Dewey, and Louie were just about grown when she stopped drinking for good; he never did. It didn't help that his lifelong profession was managing Pennsylvania State liquor stores. But the baseball cards, the gambling, the women, all the ways of spending money he didn't have: it's as if he was two different people. That shadow self, the one who lied and stole and sneaked around, just wouldn't let go. A few months sober here and there; never enough to give his liver a chance, not with hepatitis C.

Two weeks before he turned fifty, he fell down the stairs. It could have been a trip to the emergency room, a cast, something to tease him about at a family dinner. Instead it was a chance to give up. The two different people that he was agreeing at last. Fuck this. We're out.

Who Dat

died 2013

THE BAR FOR "CRAZY" is high in New Orleans. Same with "alcoholic" and "drug addict." I once heard someone there explain that he knew he didn't have a drinking problem because he stayed in on Fridays. This aspect of the city's culture made me feel right at home when I arrived in the early eighties. My New Orleans hosts were a couple of old friends who had moved down from New York State. Now they were birds of a feather in a flock of odd ducks: underground musicians, visual artists, psychics, conspiracy theorists, voodoo queens. Their main man and direct line into the indigenous New Orleans music scene was a cadaverous guitar player who, still in his twenties, was already a legend. Though his style was more experimental punk than funk or blues, his band was everywhere, opening for the Meters or Professor Longhair, backing up Earl King or Little Queenie. He was widely considered the city's best songwriter, though few could name a single song he'd written.

Little he said made logical sense, and he was impossible to pin down about anything. His eyes looked sad all the time. He had a young son and a wife, later another wife, and he was devoted to all of them. He was kind. Acutely aware of the invisible things around us, he had personal experience with alien abduction. He also had amazing drug connections. So amazing he eventually had to leave New Orleans to get away from them and wound up living in voluntary exile for the rest of his life.

One time, we stopped in Atlanta to visit him and his wife. They had a rambling, two-story house with a huge kitchen. Diane took us to the farmers' market, where I bought three bunches of Swiss chard for a pasta dish from *Sundays at Moosewood*. The details of that recipe are the thing I remember best in this whole story. *Ziti con bietole*. Try it.

Though we had been out of touch for decades, he found me on Facebook and called when he learned he was dying. He was sixty-two, diagnosed with Stage IV cancer, and since I had written about my role in Tony's assisted suicide, he wondered if I had any ideas for him. Other than that, he just wanted to say hey.

The Artist

THE FIRST TIME I saw him, 1999 was far in the future and we were as bad as we would ever be. My sister and Steve, Tony and me, high as kites at Radio City Music Hall, in our terrible eighties clothes and our big pink hair. He sang "International Lover" from a flying bed. When it was over, we found the car sitting right where we'd parked it on Fifth Avenue, despite having left the keys dangling in the door.

The next time I saw him was again with my sister. It was the new millennium, and our luck had flip-flopped several times: both the boys from the first scene were long dead, and she had ten years clean. We were with our third and second husbands in the very last row of the Meadowlands. He was far away, a five-foot-two vegan Jehovah's Witness from Minneapolis with a genius as big as the moon.

The last time I saw him was shortly after the Baltimore uprising, when he gave a concert for peace on Mother's Day. As if I knew it was my last chance, I paid $1,000 for my daughter and me to sit in the third row. The fog machine started blowing, the purple lights came up, and then they poured out one after another, the top ten on my subconscious jukebox. The swelling, melancholy chords of "Little Red Corvette," the skittering riff that starts "When Doves Cry." Ten thousand voices singing *You, I would die for you*, and it felt like something good could happen in this maddened city. I was bent over, sobbing. Mom, said my daughter. Watch the show.

I was so proud to have been born in the same year as him. Prince, Madonna, Keith Haring, Michael Jackson, and me, I used to say. Now Madonna and I are holding down the fort. I could not believe he died of an overdose until the autopsy came out. The original straight-edge, taken down by shattered hips and platform shoes. He saw it coming, had called a doctor who was on the way to take him to rehab. For weeks, I couldn't stop searching for articles about it, as if one might have a different ending.

The Young Hercules

died 2015

THE ORIGINS OF THE idea of dumping cold water on one's head to raise money for charity are unclear, says Wikipedia, but in the summer of 2014, that wacky idea went viral, and videos of the Ice Bucket Challenge were legion. Once soaked, the dripping victim would pass on the challenge, and the person named would either have to donate to ALS research or get dunked him or herself, though most did both. One of these videos now lives on the website of KSAT, a television station in San Antonio. In it, a man in a wheelchair, a man who cannot move or speak, has fourteen buckets of ice water poured on his head while his mother and his best friend address the cameras.

Unlike similar videos, which are hard to watch because of the vicarious head-freezing, this one is hard to watch because the man's limbs are wasted and his body is curled in on itself, his neck is crimped and his beard is prematurely gray. He is forty-two,

•   43   •

and he has been living with this disease for fourteen years. Using the last working muscle in his body, he can approximate a smile, and he does, briefly, with half his mouth. His eyes tell another story, electric with yearning.

He was a rock climber, a kayaker, and a wilderness guide, a fearless adventurer and a hopeless romantic poet, and he was not out of his twenties when it began. First the stumbling, the strange weakness, the trouble swallowing. Then the diagnosis, a string of terrible syllables that stood for losing everything, not just locomotion and speech but laughter and sex and beer and pushing his hair out of his eyes.

This broken young Hercules came from a line of men rooted in Wales, blessed and cursed by the stubborn belief that they could do the impossible. His grandfather had escaped from a German POW camp. His father, who was the boss at the software company I worked at in the eighties and nineties, had saved people from burning buildings, had learned whole computer languages in the course of a single weekend.

Fourteen buckets of ice water. One for each of the fourteen years. And then a smile. I hope the cruel gods were watching.

The Neatnik

I WAS TWENTY-FIVE WHEN I met her at the software company in Austin; she was thirty-two. (I only mention our ages because what I'm about to say could lead you to believe we were in high school.) She had perfectly straight, shiny, light brown hair, a sun-kissed complexion, a wide smile and big blue eyes; she wore slim jeans and a pressed Oxford button-down every day. Her handwriting was beautiful and her office impeccably organized; though I couldn't read computer languages, I can only imagine how elegant her programs were. She had grown up in Virginia—sweet Southern drawl, check—married her childhood sweetheart, and moved to Texas. Now they hosted our company parties in an airy A-frame on the wild outskirts of town. Needless to say, the spices were in alphabetical order. In a previous incarnation, she had probably invented Feng Shui.

In addition to all this, she was gentle, unassuming, kind, a very shrewd investor, and an animal lover. She meditated at her desk twice a day, which allowed her to work fourteen hours at a stretch with focus and accuracy. She and the boss, who was the company's founder, CEO, and president, were often holed up in her office coding bug fixes long into the night.

Can you even imagine the tempest in our teapot when it was revealed that the boss was splitting up with his live-in girlfriend, who also happened to be the VP, and The Neatnik was leaving her husband, childhood sweetheart turned successful attorney, so they could be together? I may have been just a tiny bit less surprised than everyone else, as a few months earlier I had seen the two of them getting out of her black Mazda RX-7 in the parking garage. Some said her marriage wasn't sailing as smoothly as it seemed. But still.

Of course there were varying opinions and conflicting loyalties. Though I felt for the VP and understood the general outrage, that it was in The Neatnik's character to have conducted this secret affair, then go public and explode her whole life—that is something I will always admire. That is love, baby.

Soon the lawyer was back in Virginia and the boss was ensconced in the A-frame. He got her into his macrobiotic obsession, but she still threw great parties, now featuring seaweed-stuffed mushrooms that took days to prepare. After the software company sold, she became a substitute teacher at the local high school. Probably Feng Shui'd the classrooms, fed everyone vegan cupcakes, and taught the kids TM.

I don't even know how to say that she died of uterine cancer less than a year after diagnosis. Partly to convince myself that it was true that she was gone, I flew down to help my boss with her memorial, held on what would have been her sixty-second birthday. One last sunset on the deck, one last margarita, or five. Oh, sweet Neatnik, goodbye.

The Velveteen Rabbit

died 2017

In our salad days, in the bloom of health and talent, early on our paths, headquarters was a sprawling stone rancher in West Austin, a long, low, Frank Lloyd Wright–looking thing that stretched out beside a turquoise pool as if it were a movie star. Inside, young women were writing poems and playing music, having long conversations that turned into romances that turned into friendships that turned into a lesbian folk-rock band that was a little bit famous at the time. She was the elfin blond in John Lennon glasses, on guitar.

I wandered into her little bedroom, walls covered with her brightly colored scritch-scratch paintings, and found her eating a hard-boiled egg. You're always eating hard-boiled eggs, I said, and she told me in her matter-of-fact tone that she had eaten only hard-boiled eggs for the past two weeks. As a young mother, very concerned about what people ate, this did not seem right to me. But asceticism came to her naturally.

So did anger. Hypersensitivity. The first gnawings of mania and delusion. A group house, a democratically run band, a hazy poolside bacchanal could only last so long. She made two records by herself, but as the years went by, the static in her head drowned out everything. The salad days were long past when some of the old friends learned she was living in a storage unit. The bandmates gave a fund-raiser; another couple took her in. Eat, they begged her, sleep, take your medicine. Instead, she would tear off on some frantic mission, winding up in the hospital when bystanders called 911.

When death came to her at sixty-one, alone in a rented room, I had not spoken to her in more than twenty years. But always with me has been one of her beautiful-mind paintings; she probably traded it for a couple of haircuts from my husband. A wide, black frame is painted around an intricate, kaleidoscopically colored-in doodle. Part of it appears to be a psychedelic hardboiled egg, its yolk exploding with arrows and shazam lines into its white, which is orange. Around the image in a careful square she lettered a line from a children's story. *For where the tear had fallen a flower grew out of the ground, a mysterious flower, not at all like any that grew in the garden.*

The Werewolf

died 2013

AT PARTIES BY THE turquoise pool, eating pescado Veracruz and drinking Mexican beer, her friends have no idea. He's a little quiet for this boho crowd, but so is she. She is watching him tip a bottle to his lips, and she is afraid.

If you have never seen one, you may not believe in werewolves. You don't know what can happen to a honey-haired boy from Chicago after the third glass of whiskey and the seventh beer. Even after you see it once, how the cold gleam comes into his eye, how his voice becomes a howl, how his hands curve into fists, even after you wake up sickened, covered with bites and bruises, you still tell yourself there's no such thing as werewolves. Or, my husband is not a werewolf.

The first strange thing she noticed was how much he hated stoplights, how he struggled with a little yellow box trying to tell him what to do. Then it began in earnest, and continued in secrecy. Even though she had seen the old clumps of fur around the house when they visited his parents, she still imagined he would change.

One morning she woke with another kind of nausea, the kind that means birth control has let you down. Having a baby with a werewolf is quite a risk, but she gave him this last chance. Briefly, he was wide-eyed and sheepish with tenderness. Then came the night when he was not. Her friends arrived and loaded her and her daughter into their pickup, and that was the end of it.

The next woman was smarter. When he bought a gun, when he violated his restraining order, she called the police. After that, the werewolf was locked up for a while. When he got out, it wasn't long before he fell down drunk and hit his head. Went to bed with a headache and never woke up. There's a honey-haired boy from Chicago who might have agreed: it was a blessing.

The Queen of the Scene
died 2017

I MET HER AT a strip club called the Doll House. She was one of the Jam and Jelly Girls, bodacious backup singers in tutus who did burlesque routines with Dino Lee and his White Trash Revue. Tony and I elbowed our way backstage to introduce ourselves—as she herself was a famous groupie, we figured she'd understand. About five years later, she became my editor at the *Austin Chronicle*, and the last time I remember seeing her was in 1996, after Tony died and I wrote a book about it. She was in the studio audience at my stupid *Oprah* appearance. Her first husband was gay, as were her father and brother, so she fit into the theme for the show, which was "Holy shit, I think this man is a homosexual."

After sleeping with many rock stars, she began her writing career with a gossip column in the *Austin Chronicle* and quickly became its top music critic. By the time of her retirement at sixty, she was beloved as the patron saint, den mother, historian, and emcee of the whole scene. She went on to conduct what may have been the most glamorous, enviable, poignant, and lengthy death in history, which you could attend from afar on Facebook, with the city naming a park after her and legions of musicians and writers offering tributes in the months before she died.

She had several great loves, the last being a treasured Austin hash-slinger named Steve, and though they had about five minutes before she got sick, it was a damn fine romance. You know what, let me give her the mic. *On a cold February day in early 2013, I told my boyfriend and my mother that something was wrong with me and I needed to go to the emergency room. I went into surgery the next morning and upon recovery was given a terminal diagnosis of Stage IV colon cancer. That quick, that fast. It's a cruel luxury to know death will come soon, but it's a bizarre comfort to know how.*

A life writing about music wasn't part of the plan, but then I'd had no plan. I've long joked that I got in through the back door, so whenever I am let in through the front door, I run to the back to see who I can let in.

The Volunteer

died 2013

AFTER MY COMMENTARY ABOUT Tony's death aired on *All Things Considered*, I got quite a pile of condolence cards, one of which I remember down to the blue ink and the folded note paper. Direct and full of feeling, it was from a stranger whose son had died young because of drugs. I wrote back, telling her I was writing a memoir, and she wrote back telling me she was organizing a literary event.

My correspondent turned out to be the founder of the Texas Book Festival, an open-minded, down-to-earth woman whose generosity was legendary. After my reading from *First Comes Love* at the festival, she brought someone over to meet me at the book table—her friend and cofounder, Laura Bush. Laura bought a copy of the book for each of her twins for their fifteenth birthdays. This definitely made me rethink Laura Bush, and if you ever read it, you will, too.

While running this book festival would have been enough for most people, the cause of literature had to share The Volunteer with the causes of wildflowers, freedom of speech, health care, public art, historic buildings, cancer research, the advancement of women and minorities, and a small army of people she individually mother-henned. All were at a loss when cancer stole her at seventy-three.

Another writer told me how The Volunteer had flown to her aid when her teenage son was having difficulties. These troubles were private, of course, but every town is a small town where such things are concerned. This writer and The Volunteer were at the book festival, heading to her reading, when they were accosted by a vaguely familiar woman. Why hello! she cried. Har yew? As the writer hesitated, the woman launched into her exciting news. USC and Stanford were fighting over her son! You know Billy, don't you? He plays lacrosse! But what about your boy?

The writer gave her a small smile. He's still finding his path, she said.

Oh?

At this point, The Volunteer put her arm around the writer and started walking. Honey, when a mother tells you her son is still finding his path, she called over her shoulder, that's the end of the discussion.

She could start a real conversation or end a fake one with a single sentence. That's time management.

The All-American
died 2014

HAVING NOW SPENT MORE of my adult life single than married, I have collected quite a treasure chest of kindnesses from other's people's husbands. Put that credit card away. We'll pick you up in twenty minutes. You girls sit down; I'll do the dishes. One or another of these guys has helped me arrange everything from my fortieth birthday party to my divorce, has dealt with my flooded basement, my dying computer, and my incompatible video format, has stood with me against egregious invoices, evil lawsuits, and greedy charlatans. And then there was the very much bigger problem, my sons' father having died when they were six and four.

The silver lining of this tragedy was collectively provided by an all-pro team of loaner dads: two gourmet journalists, a conservative lawyer, a Cajun partier, a bipolar (but very sweet) neighbor, and a Texas outdoorsman: from a big Italian family in a small town, the kind of guy who still got together to throw the football and drink beers with his fraternity brothers, still a big kid himself. So tall, dark, and handsome, he could have played that guy on TV.

With a rare lack of snark, he and his wife split up when our kids were in preschool; he moved two blocks away to a townhouse overlooking the creek. His son, my son, and a third Musketeer would plan elaborate expeditions from our house to his, through the reeds, over the footbridge, up the incline to the apartment where he would cook them a he-man dinner of steak and spinach. Popeye the sailor man in his teeny bachelor kitchen. Not for long, though. There was a lovely blonde at work who had once announced during a discussion of engagement rings that she didn't want one at all; she would marry the man who gave her a fishing rod. One day he showed up at an office happy hour with a large, oddly shaped bag from the sporting goods store.

Fourteen years later, she found him in his armchair in front of the History Channel, still flashing its battlefields and galleons. He was fifty-six, just like my own father who died the same way: the heart in the dark of the night that loses its place. Like me, his son was out of the nest by then. Old enough to know how lucky we were.

The Paid Professional Codependent

THAT WAS WHAT SHE called herself, the woman with the gorgeous red hair and big black sunglasses who picked me up at the airport for the Bay Area portion of my book tour. She looked more like a country rock star than a media escort. In fact, she was both, as well as a radio producer, a columnist, and the organizer of the Rock Bottom Remainders, the famous-author band of Stephen King, Amy Tan, Dave Barry, et al. Why do you think I bothered writing a book at all, if not to become a go-go dancer for this band? On the way to my first interview that morning, we stopped for espresso at a place with Latin music. Watch this, I told her, leaping from my stool to demonstrate my hip-swiveling abilities.

Essentially, a media escort is your best friend for one day. And just one day with this best friend was all I needed. The Rock Bottom Remainders had a show coming up over Memorial Day weekend at a book-sellers conference at the Hollywood Palladium, and somehow this stop got added to my tour and I ended up onstage performing with all of the above, plus Roy Blount, Matt Groening, Cynthia Heimel, and Bruce Springsteen. Who else could have done this for me but her? But she would do more. The next time I went on a book tour, a couple years later, I had dragged my food-writer boyfriend along and it was my birthday and unbelievably we found out in the middle of it that one of our best friends had committed suicide. What a day that was. Thank God we had a paid professional codependent, the best in the business, to get us through it.

It was shocking to read that she had died of breast cancer at sixty-three. Her sixty-three was most people's forty. According to the *New York Times*, she was surrounded by authors, among them Ms. Tan, Mr. Barry, Ms. Angelou. Ms. Collins called on the phone and sang "Amazing Grace."

The Southern Writer

died 2012

IN THE HEAD-SPINNING MIDDLE nineties, I was occasionally sent by my publisher to stay in hotel suites with doorbells, to be driven around by escorts, and to speak at fancy events, like a charity fund-raiser in Bloomington, Indiana. There I found myself one spring afternoon in the back of a limo with three other writers: a bestselling women's author, a courtly scrivener out of Mississippi, and another young beginner like me. Having never before met such a successful colleague, I had many questions for the grande dame, and she answered them graciously. Once again this year, she told us, she was missing the blooming of her lilies because of her book tour. She had begged Michael Korda—her dear friend—to change the schedule, but there's only one good time of year to publish a blockbuster. I asked her about her daughter, also a famous writer with three names. Three Names was one of five children, we learned, raised while their young widowed mother, not yet a famous author, flew around the world as a stewardess for Pan Am.

Admirably, The Southern Writer, who wore lime green socks, and the beginner, a sweet-looking blonde, maintained strict poker faces throughout this interview.

Diving into The Southern Writer's book after I got home, I found some of the most wonderful sentences I'd ever read, retelling one of the nastiest episodes in American history. The Southern Writer had grown up in the town where Emmett Till was lynched, and had been thinking about it for a good half century when he published this book. It recounts the story from multiple viewpoints, including the eye of the dead boy, weaving into the tragedy a skein of outrageous humor, largely created by his delicious use of language. Something about his writing evokes the blues, and it worked in the same way the blues does, making something beautiful out of evil and pain.

More than ten years later, when I was working at a low-residency MFA in Pittsburgh, a visiting author was rolled in in a wheelchair. I was squinting at him, thinking, Wait, don't I know this guy? Marion Winik, he drawled. How wonderful to see you. At sixty-five, he was crippled and prematurely aged by a painful nerve disease, but his demeanor was as genial as ever and his memory obviously working better than mine. Here we were at yet another literary event, he pointed out, while our lilies bloomed at home unseen.

After he died, I read passionate remembrances by other authors and former students. There was nobody who didn't wish they'd had more time with him. Though he did not publish until his mid-forties, there were seven books I hadn't read yet. Our relationship was really just beginning.

The Belle of the Ball

died 2012

IN BETWEEN MY FIRST marriage and my second, a big green-eyed food writer with wavy hair and a mustache caught my eye. One day I was discussing the pros and cons of this guy with my good friend when her mother, an exquisitely preserved woman of seventy-some with sparkling eyes to match her sparkling jewelry, spoke up. That's a good-lookin' man, she said in her deep Texas drawl. If you don't want him, I'll take him.

As a girl who loved to dance, my friend's mother had in her youth dated some fine young fellows; what she loved most was to drive into Austin or San Antonio to see Duke Ellington or Count Basie. I was wild, she later conceded, but I had high standards. It was interesting when, at twenty-one, she returned from business college to marry the man who later became my friend's daddy. This was a man who didn't dance at all, and didn't exactly have a profession, either. Since her mother was about to take over the town credit union, the money thing wasn't an issue, but how did The Belle of the Ball marry a man who didn't dance?

My friend got an inkling when in her early adolescence, she was given the sex talk by her daddy, who had been put in charge of most of the upbringing while her mother was at work. When he explained the situation to her, she said, That sounds like it hurts. He said, Oh yeah, at first. After that, you'll be chasin' him around the room to get your hands on him.

These days, my friend and I love to raise a glass to our mothers, both of whom loved to raise a glass. We discuss their fashion convictions: her mother's went right down to the skin. If she wore a pink dress, you could be certain she was also wearing a pink bra, pink slip, and pink panties. She had a drawerful of filmy nightgowns to sleep in and even in her nineties would not put on a pair of pajamas without a little lace on them. Neither my friend nor I ever dressed properly, and we were often told as much by our mothers. Yet we both know how it feels to have a very particular woman with whom you didn't always see eye to eye admire how you turned out and what you've accomplished. It's pink silk lingerie for your soul.

The Rancher

died 2012

My Texas-sized crush on the state of Texas, founded in Austin circa 1976, got its spacious western annex in 1988, when a good friend took Tony and me and our six-month-old baby out to visit her mother in Odessa, a six-hour drive that took four in her BMW. They were a family of cattle ranchers, her mother the sixth generation, and they still owned a nice-sized piece of the Permian Basin, though they'd given a chunk away to build the university. My friend's childhood residence was a beautiful, relaxed family home, not overly formal as such a place might be up in Yankeeland. There was a mezzanine that ran around the second floor, and I could picture her three older brothers racing around it with their chaps and pop-guns.

We couldn't wait to strip off our infant son's diaper and put him in the hot tub, a plan my friend's mother—perfectly coiffed and dressed, yet somehow slightly, endearingly gawky—at first found alarming.

But when she came out to check on us, she was tickled to death. Why, look at that! she said, blinking her big brown eyes. He's practically swimming! And every time that boy's name came up for the next twenty years, my friend's mother would proudly recall that he was the smartest baby she had ever seen.

As much as I loved anything about the Lone Star State, I loved this family, their stories, their accents, their cooking, their generosity, their incredibly good taste in clothes and furnishings and art. For years, my greatest joy was to be invited to the birthday party my friend and her mother threw themselves every other year at the Gage Hotel, out in the great nowhere bordering Big Bend National Park, where we would drink margaritas and eat Mexican food and dance under the stars for two days.

I'm having such a hard time getting to the sad part—maybe that's her doing. To bury two sons in two years, to struggle so long with that damn disease taking everything you have left—Shh, y'all hush now, she says. Come over here and look at this sunset. Is that not the most beautiful sky you've ever seen?

The Father of the Bride

died 2012

HE IS SLIM, STRAIGHT, and smiling in a black tuxedo jacket; she is a cloud of organza, a single pale hand resting on his upturned palm. These two have been practicing this dance since before she could read. Off to the right, fine young men in bow ties stand like a barbershop quartet, arms outstretched, mouths wide. *Waltz across Texas with you in my arms, waltz across Texas with you.* The one with the boutonniere has just become her husband.

By the time I met her at the software company, that wedding photo had become a painting above the grand piano on the wall of her living room. Behind the bridal mufti, she had perfect posture, a steel-trap mind, and a no-bullshit attitude; he was an excellent if not very humble writer who barricaded the house during football games. There were many good parties there, but the marriage had no more luck than his Houston Oilers, and before long the song we were dancing to was "D-I-V-O-R-C-E" by Tammy Wynette. My friend's daddy danced at her wedding, he danced at her divorce party, and he'd dance at her next wedding, too. Whatever makes you happy, honey. You go right ahead.

My friend's father was from a town that no longer exists called Concrete, Texas. He grew up speaking German, picking cotton, plowing fields, and riding a horse to school. Then siphoning gas out of the tractor to start the truck. His mama got one of those female cancers and died when he was fourteen; long after he grew into his Stetson, he still wept to think of it. By then he could talk to anybody about anything, sell them a mule, beat them at poker, and congenially mispronounce their name throughout their entire acquaintance. He taught three daughters to dance; my friend was the baby.

But I don't know how, I protested the first time my friend grabbed my hand for a two-step. Pshaw, she said, steering me out on the floor. For a hapless East Coast shimmy-shaker like myself, dancing with these people is like embracing a moving tree. You just hang on to the branches as they dip and whirl. Don't be fooled by the cloud of organza—the girl in that painting has all her daddy's moves. All the time he was training her to follow, he taught her to lead.

Portrait of a Lady

died 2017

MOTHER ABHORRED VIOLENCE, MY pal from East Texas begins. Probably because the love of her life, her first husband, died in World War II. Then her second husband, my brother's dad, knocked her teeth out. My father, who was ten years older than she was, was an alcoholic womanizer. You know, the type that would go out for a loaf of bread and come back Tuesday.

I was four and my brother fifteen the night he picked up a couple of floozies in a honky-tonk in Kilgore, she continues. They convinced him to drive them to Dallas to party, then stole his cash and his car and threw him out on the side of the highway. He walked to the nearest house and asked to use the phone. The operator who connected his call turned out to be his niece. What happened, Uncle Carl? she asked.

I got rolled by barflies on the Dallas highway, he said. Tell Larse—that was his twin brother—to come get me.

He had planned to tell my mother a brawl had broken out at the sawmill, but by the time he got home, it was too late. Get the hell out, Mother said.

Well, Judy, he answered calmly. I need a shower. And some supper.

She picked up the .22 and aimed it at him. My brother grabbed me as he went for cover. Later he explained: you always want to be behind the one with the gun. A shot cracked, and a bullet zinged into the wall over the refrigerator.

Yep, said my dad. I'll be in the shower.

Two years later he died of a heart attack, then she married Jim. Jim never laid a hand on her in fifty years. Mother carried a pistol in her apron all her life, just in case of intruders, but as far as I know she never shot a living thing. She was a nurse, and an animal lover. Every morning she went down to the creek with a china cup of coffee and her dogs, maybe the llama, a few cows, a chicken or two. The mockingbirds, she said, were the most social of the birds. Her favorite to see was the heron.

After their mother's death, my friend and her brother walked along the creek one last time. They kept stumbling over china cups. As they were leaving, she hung one in a tree.

The Statistic

died 2018

IN THE MONTHS IMMEDIATELY following her mother's death, my pal from East Texas really got clobbered. One of her oldest friends committed suicide; another, a powerhouse who'd been a speechwriter for Ann Richards, was treated successfully for cancer—then died. Next came an even lower blow. A guy she saw every day, another East Texan, a work friend who ended up becoming much more.

He was a wild child, no doubt, but these days it was down to getting a little carried away at office parties. He was forty, with two kids and a job he loved. He would do anything for people he cared about, and he cared about everyone.

The guys got a house in the French Quarter for a bachelor party. Started with a long day of barhopping. Somebody knew somebody knew somebody who could get some coke. For old times' sake. Three of them left the club and went back to the house. While one met the dealer in the front room, the wild child and the other guy waited out back. The exchange was made; the dealer left. Before he called in his friends to get started, the guy took a little taste. Whoa. Nuh-uh. He ran out the front door and down the street to catch the dealer before he got away. Left the baggie on the counter.

By the time he got back, there were two bodies on the floor. Thirteen hours later, the other guy woke up from his coma. The wild child never did. My friend went to New Orleans to say goodbye. The doctor told her fentanyl—so much cheaper to fill a baggie with than cocaine—causes fifteen deaths every month at that hospital alone.

How do you say stop, enough?

Right. You can't.

Two Slips of the Knife

died 2008, 2012

FORGIVE ME FOR PUTTING two of them together, as if I could lure this story once and for all into a very small pen, shut the gate, and run away. It's the one where the highway and the weather, the big cars and the tiny errors steal her forever, our precious golden girl with a heart full of good. One was a sixteen-year-old on her way to a birthday party, a dear, down-to-earth philosopher-tomboy who loved summer camp and golf. One was a twenty-year-old driving to her job at Francesca's at the mall, saving for a move to Montana. She was an artist, a dog lover, and a tree hugger, the beloved baby of her family. They both were. And their mothers—one my sister-mom in Texas, one my student in an MFA program in Pittsburgh—got the same phone call. The one where they tell you there was nothing that could be done.

After the moment when nothing could be done came the avalanche of doing. People sent messages and placed phone calls and made pots of chili and bought boxes of scones. They pushed back the furniture, filled plastic cups with forks and spoons. They went to the drugstore, they booked airline tickets, they went through photographs. They went to buy tissues, retrieved crumpled tissues, pulled white tissues like doves from the box. Some people were just doing their jobs: conducting investigations, delivering flowers. Finally all that was over, and everyone went away. Back to their unharmed children, their familiar tasks and uncomplicated conversations, back to the world where even the T-shirts insist life is good.

Oh my sweet ladies, friends of my heart! Broken like a vase or a bone or a car, broken beyond full repair or even the desire for it. If you wait long enough, I've heard, the pain somehow eases. Very slightly, very slowly, one notch at a time. I will be there, I swear. I want to see.

The Old Rake
died 2017

TEXAS LOVES ITS LEGENDS, and he was a legendary Texas legend-maker, a hard-living gonzo journalist from an oil town called Royalty, famous for articles about sports figures and strippers. *On the road home to Brownwood in her green '74 Cadillac with the custom upholstery and the CB radio, clutching a pawn ticket for her $3,000 mink, Candy Barr thought about biscuits.* A heart attack, he explained after he survived one, felt *like a bear sitting on your chest reading the sports page.*

I read him long before I met him, and the only time I spent with him was when we all went to Venice for a wedding, during which he played an unwitting role in a moment that changed my life. He was with his third wife, a real estate agent who would soon help me sell my last place of residence in Texas. I was with the man I would leave it all and move to Pennsylvania for, starry-eyed in love. During a layover on the way back, my sweetheart recalled my attention to a good-night kiss I had given this writer in a hotel bar. He had seen the twinkle in the old man's eye, and he had a pretty good idea what it meant. Oh, Jesus. What it meant was that the clock on this marriage was already ticking; the first green shoots of the plant that would strangle us had already poked through.

Which is not to say the guy wasn't trouble. He was not good to wives, as his third wife's best friend put it. After the fourth one left him, he finally had to learn to work the dishwasher. One day in his early eighties, he fell coming out of the shower. He lay there for four days before someone found him, then died a week later in the hospital surrounded by old friends drinking tequila out of Styrofoam cups.

That sounds like a story he could have written. Funny thing is, his editor had recently asked him to keep a "death journal," a diary that would run in the magazine after he was gone. A final farewell, a macabre honor—but this old pro saw the flaw in the plan. How you gonna pay me? he said.

The Mother of Four
died 2008

My SECOND MARRIAGE TOOK me from Austin, Texas, to rural Pennsylvania, leaving a twenty-year cache of friendships and a house near the neighborhood school for a hermit husband in a place so isolated I had to drive my kids to the bus stop. The only people he knew were his former neighbors, and the only reason he knew them is because he'd had to go over and tell them their barn was on fire. They were a family of six, and they hadn't been in the area long. This meant they socialized with people they weren't related to and were not afraid to try my spicy Thai noodles. Then my son formed a band with their son and I spent much of the next six years sitting in their kitchen. We were moms: we loved our chardonnay.

Our friendship had a certain counterintuitive magic. She was six years younger, with perfect nails and makeup, and tailored slacks—like a stewardess from the sixties or a dreamy first-grade teacher. She was

Catholic, Republican, and pro-life, had married and had her first baby around twenty. When she told people we were like sisters, I felt a blush of pride. We had some fine times together as groupie moms, the two of us in our T-shirts at the so-called gigs, gingerly swaying due to our various back and knee troubles.

When her back troubles led to surgery, when the surgery didn't work, when it turned out the back pain had only been camouflaging the kidney cancer—by then she had been in bed for months and it was too late. My mother was dying in New Jersey, my marriage was in freefall, my forty-three-year-old friend was in mortal agony: there wasn't enough chardonnay or Vicodin in the world. I relentlessly cooked Thai noodles and pot roast and spaghetti, and I drove around in circles dropping them off.

So much of motherhood turns out to be about letting go. The way she had to do it, all at once and much too soon, is unimaginable and impossible and happened anyway. Eight years after her funeral, I saw her beautiful children assembled at her daughter's wedding. Never have I seen more clearly how my world will go on without me.

The Man of Honor
died 2009

Dear Marion, The purpose of this email is to tell you that my son, a former student of yours and your ex-husband's, drowned around midnight on August 17 while canoeing under a full moon on Lake Champlain in Grand Isle, Vermont. Earlier that day, he had been man of honor for his sister at her wedding.

The ceremony was absolutely beautiful, outdoors in a little cove on the lake. Afterward, my son, who lived nearby in a cottage with his girlfriend, had invited two friends to spend the night. We planned to drive them home if they had too much to drink, but he hadn't. He took his job as man of honor seriously. We still asked him to call us when he got home, as parents tend to do.

He called our hotel, I answered, and I told him to enjoy the night with his friends and check out the beautiful full moon. I went to bed thinking all was right with the world. Around 1 a.m. we got the hysterical call from his girlfriend. As soon as she said the boat had capsized, I knew it would not have a good outcome. We drove back the twenty miles, we got lost on the island, Sarah kept calling in tears. When we finally got there, there were lights all over. Ambulance, police, media, helicopter, boats up and down the shoreline . . . the dive team came at daylight.

Today I was trying to remember important people in his life who might want to know about what happened. His two years at Penn State Harrisburg were quite lackluster, except for the two of you, and the man who owned the hot wing place up in the Poconos where he worked. He ended up in Vermont, where he lived with his sister, and became a brewer at Magic Hat, a job that he loved. They loved him too. I hear they are going to bronze his brewing boots and keep them on display at the brewhouse. Marion, I am not sure if you remember my son, but I felt the need to let you know, just in case you do.

The Little Bird

died 2016

I HAD MY LAST baby at forty-two, having just moved to a big house in the middle of nowhere. While everyone in the family got a life, I remained depressed and friendless through my pregnancy. Sure, the birth of my daughter was a brief pick-me-up; then I was desperate for a sitter. The headline Beautiful Blond Baby on my sign on the grocery store bulletin board drew the attention of a mother with just such an infant in her cart. She was a tall drink of water, a chatty Texas blonde.

And so the beautiful blond babies became a pair, cared for by the tall drink of water, who was full of pep and enthusiasm for talking toys and cut-up apples and playground slides, even after she got pregnant with her second child. She read them Christian storybooks featuring a cast of vegetables and took them down the street to a playgroup at the church. Her daughter, already tall and skinny at three, began to show a gift for mischief. Unmaking all the beds to build a fort. Sprinkling talcum powder over a second-floor railing to make it snow. Doing gymnastics on the shower curtain rod of a newly renovated bathroom.

By the time the girls were eleven, both of us had moved away and my relationship with this mom was down to mass messages and holiday portraits. Then we received an email sent from a hospital waiting room. *She is wearing a bandanna now most of the time, even at home. When she takes it off she looks like a little bird. It is like she is reverting back to being a baby, when no one could see her hairs except me and John. If she will allow it, I will get her a haircut after her CT at the hospital salon. But she may just want to go home.*

Five years of treatment followed, with just a few short interludes of hope. Though she never really got to be a teenager, she died at sixteen. After a few dark, empty months, her mother returned to babysitting, making up energetic outdoor games and doing puzzles with the preschoolers of her neighborhood. She doesn't send out so many mailings anymore, but on last year's Christmas card, her son, now fourteen, holds up a photo of his sister, who looks like a little bird. My own beautiful baby, no longer so blond, brought it in from the mailbox, eyes shining.

The Montessori Teacher
died 2014

AFTER MY DAUGHTER'S YEAR at the Christian pre-school in Central Pennsylvania, I was delighted to find out there was a Montessori up the road in Jacobus, which also featured an Amish butcher and a fishing supply. The school was run by a mother-daughter team, an appealing yet unlikely pair. The mother was a put-together blonde who wore wool suits and taught fractions to toddlers using a special set of blocks called the Pink Tower. The daughter, Miss Nancy, was nearly a foot taller than her mom, big and soft, with dark, bushy curls and eyes like an Italian movie star. Miss Nancy had a special-needs son the same age as my daughter. She was clearly the most nurturing person in the world.

T, T, TLC. Mon-te, Montessori! We love eve-ry-bo-dy, at TLC Montessori. I had composed a long ballad about the school, which I sang to my daughter at bedtime, adding verses for each teacher, aide, and playmate.

What a joy it was to find something to sing about in this place that had turned me into a perpetual kvetch machine.

Not long after we moved away, Miss Nancy's brother died in a motorcycle accident. Her mother took an indefinite leave of absence; Miss Nancy carried on. But one evening six years later, she got home from work and rushed into the house—a ringing phone? a bursting bladder? a boy with a nosebleed?—accidentally leaving her car running in the garage. Steadily, the colorless, odorless carbon monoxide gas seeped into the house; she and her son very likely went to bed with headaches. In the morning, both of them were found dead in their beds, each with one of the dogs. What her mother did after that I do not know.

I have looked up the directions for using the Pink Tower, which consists of ten pink wooden cubes, increasing in volume by powers of three: 1, 8, 27, 64, and so on. To begin, tell the child you have something to show him. Say: for this lesson, we will need a mat. Have him fetch and unroll a mat. Then bring him over to the Pink Tower. Say: this is the Pink Tower.

This is the Pink Tower. It is something even a child can understand.

The Ambassador's Wife

THE MOTHER-IN-LAW OF MY second marriage, an
actress and a writer whose place in my life has long
outlasted the bond that connected us, lives in the
shadow of the Blue Ridge Mountains in Rappahan-
nock County. Back in the seventies and eighties, this
county of Virginia farmers filled with retirees from
Washington, D.C.; with refugees from the Foreign
Service; with artists and artisans; with older women
who didn't color their gray, far ahead of the trend.
Among the interesting and distinguished characters
in my mother-in-law's circle was a woman from all
three groups: an ambassador's wife, a brilliant painter,
an older mother of three with a troubled marriage.
She had lived many years in Kazakhstan, St. Peters-
burg, and Moscow and was particularly known for her
luminous Central Asian faces. I met her once, when
we were all going to a show at the town's little theater. She offered to have my little girl stay with her
daughter at their house, looked after by her twenty-

something son. I remember the family as three gentle souls, all a bit anxious. The painter had spent time in an institution not long before.

My mother-in-law owned a large painting this woman had done for her, a nearly life-sized Russian peasant who ruled over the entrance to the kitchen. Wearing a blue-and-white dress and flowered scarf around her head, she watches the viewer with blue eyes and an almost-smile. Her wooden table, shown in flattened perspective, holds a bowl of borscht and all its ingredients: beets, cabbage, carrots, garlic, bay leaves, scallions, and salt. The canvas has a decorated border, and there are two beets floating in the air that resemble hearts. I loved how this painting was also a recipe, the same recipe I used myself, and how the image so dominated the small farmhouse that when you visited my mother-in-law, you felt you were also visiting this lady.

The year the artist killed herself, my mother-in-law sold the painting to help her granddaughter pay her college tuition. The buyer was kind enough to tell her it was worth double what she was asking and pay her the true value. As much as I might have hoped to get my hands on it someday, I didn't mind. By now, the artist's daughter must be going to college herself. It is difficult to imagine what her life has been like. Perhaps she has paid her tuition the same way.

The Playwright
died 2008

SHE WAS NOT A woman one ever saw with a computer or a cell phone, a curly-haired earth goddess in fringed scarves and jingly jewelry, a devotee of travels in India and rain dances, of storytelling and Kathakali. She liked her art forms as old as fire. Yet when I summon her via Internet mumbo jumbo, she appears. One site lists ten plays she wrote, among them this Obie winner from 1971: *A panel of two blacks and two whites is brought together, representing four points of view on America's racial problem, but before the discussion is concluded, a riot breaks out in the theatre.* And look, here she is on YouTube, singing with her composer husband the year she died. He smiles at her encouragingly, playing his guitar. She is a wasted husk of herself, two days after surgery. This thin, off-key sound is not her real voice. Okay, enough of this séance.

Have you heard the story of how she got that husband? Once upon a time, a hippie playwright who had won a theater prize in New York decided it was time to get married. There were five men in the running. She went and visited all of them. One was too fat, one was too thin, one was too rich, one was too poor. One was just right: a musician, a man who loved women, a man who lived in the shadow of the Blue Ridge. Instead of children, they had followers and protégées. They gave workshops and made records and put on shows.

What happens when an earth goddess gets uterine cancer? Eastern medicine, Western medicine, no medicine. If I had been her daughter, I might have fought her on these decisions. But I would have been wrong, because she lived as long as anyone can reasonably stand under the circumstances. Just as useful as any toxic treatment was the flock of white origami birds the followers hung in her house. She wrote her own ending, in her own bed, with her own hair. The End.

The Belligerent Stream

buried 1962

EVERYONE WHO DRIVES INTO Baltimore is shocked to discover that the interstate—a part of I-83 known as the JFX—stops dead and disappears in the middle of town. Whether you are coming from the north or the south, your route into the city will dump you off near the Inner Harbor and leave you to wend your way through downtown traffic. Before the JFX vanishes, it wanders through town like a drunk, swerving drastically left, then right, for no apparent reason.

But there is a reason. This road is built right on top of the Jones Falls, which once burbled through town to the bay, a "belligerent stream" according to early twentieth-century historian Letitia Stockett, who taught at the high school my daughter now attends. Perhaps because it was always prone to flooding and filled with trash, few mourned in the 1960s when the tough little waterway was paved over, sacrificed to suburbanites' need for speed. The alternative was tearing down buildings and slicing through neighborhoods. On the other hand, if they had finished the road as planned, the Inner Harbor would now be covered with concrete ramps. A terrible thought indeed. Though it didn't look like much back then, the decaying port has since become the city's sparkly little Disneyland; all of Baltimore most tourists ever see.

Meanwhile, the belligerent stream has never submitted entirely, as I learned recently while reading a novel set in Baltimore with a secret waterfall. I immediately emailed the author: Where is this? In the abandoned industrial neighborhood beneath the elevated part of the highway, he wrote back, look for an overgrown trail. Once we found it, my daughter had to help me down the steep makeshift steps to the rickety deck. And there it was: the surprisingly emerald waters of the Jones Falls, bursting out of the culvert, rushing to a rounded cliff, tumbling over and pounding noisily into a pool. Graffiti adds a caption to the postcard: PERSISTENCE IS KEY.

The Southern Gentleman

died 2012

I MET HIM MANY years after he changed his whole life: he quit drinking, came out, and left his wife in a single day. Sitting in the audience at his book signing, I instantly loved him; he had a deep, luscious Georgia accent, a courtly manner, and a wicked sense of humor. I rushed right up to start telling him my life story, eager to begin our friendship without delay. Soon I was on the guest list for his many gatherings. Dinnah will be ready in one ow-ah and fawty-fahv minutes, he would say at the door. Finally at the table, he blessed the food and his guests and always, last of all, the *New York Times*.

He was rarely on time for anything, spent money as if he had a trust fund, wrote slowly, lusted randily, and could always be counted on for special requests in restaurants. Ah'd lahk it *molten*, he'd tell the waiter, sending a piece of chocolate cake back to be microwaved. At his regular spots, his ice water arrived at the table with eight slices of lemon. They know me heah, he explained. As at the apartment, dinner took hours. Then he drove me home in his old boat of a car, airily bouncing, then noisily crunching over every bump.

At the time he learned he had Lou Gehrig's disease, I was pretty sick myself, about to finally start the yearlong treatment that cured me of hepatitis C. At first, it was fun to complain together, but that wore off. Soon nobody could understand him but his daughter. The last time I saw him leave the house, he had invited me to go to a production of *The Rocky Horror Picture Show*. He sat stoically in his neck brace as half-naked cast members shimmied and shook inches from his face. Some people should really keep their clothes on in public, he remarked as we left.

Even that night, making our interminable way back to the parking garage, there was something magical about him, a rare combination of chivalry, joie de vivre, and ease. Being his friend was like some kind of painless cosmetic surgery, leaving you just a little prettier and more interesting than you were before.

. . . .

THE BALTIMORE BOOK OF THE DEAD • 93

The Squash Player

I MET HER BECAUSE she was madly in love with her upstairs neighbor in the apartment building, the dashing, handsome, totally gay Southern Gentleman. The first mention of her in my inbox is him telling me—typos galore, he's already failing—that she's brought red roses for the party he's having that night, the last big one. The two of them with their sprightly gatherings! What with that creaky old elevator and its upholstered bench, you felt you were going to a cocktail party in the 1940s. Her "salon" involved a potluck hors d'oeuvre spread on her mahogany table, deviled eggs, smoked salmon on brown bread, and a generous open bar. She drank martinis, but you have whatever you want, dear. The walls were crimson, covered with paintings.

She had once been the top-seeded women's squash player in Maryland, but now she was the skinny, kooky old lady with bad hips and a fluffy dog, whom she took everywhere, as if Baltimore were Paris, and several months a year they would go to the real Paris, where I assume she met with less resistance when taking him to restaurants and theaters. Fucking A! she would say, if they wouldn't admit the dog, and throw her tickets in the trash and go home.

Despite her jaunty air and festive urges, there was something desperate about her. She was lonely and secretive, deeply miserable about growing old. I did not fully grasp this until the night I arrived in her lobby with a plate of tuna canapés and no one answered the buzzer. Then I saw the note taped to the door: our hostess had been hospitalized. A few months later, she failed at suicide for the third time, destroying her liver and kidneys. A committee went to the hospital to beg the doctors to let her go.

I had many questions, but most of them would never be answered. I did learn, at the cocktail party held in her apartment instead of a funeral, that she had appointed guardians and left a bequest for the care of her dog. Which led to the realization that, despite certain worrisome similarities, I am far luckier than she. I was never an athlete, I have no secrets, and I would not in a million years leave the dog.

Her Son

died 2017

ONE DAY MY NEIGHBOR took me with her to something called a shooting response. It was just a couple of
miles from our house, on a corner in East Baltimore.
Right there, a few days earlier, a high school senior
had been shot in the face, though there was nothing in
the backpack the killers took but a change of clothes.
Now there were sixty people assembled, friends, family, neighbors, teachers, and members of an organiza-
tion called MOMS, Mothers of Murdered Sons and
Daughters. This Baltimore-based association is open
to all: whether your child is killed by the cops, the
dealers, the gangs, or the racists, you can join.

People brought boxes of white candles and Mylar bal-
loons. They taped photos to a brick wall and placed
tea lights on the sidewalk. Then his mother, a young
woman with a turned-up nose and gold highlights in
her long, loopy waves, arrived, and they handed her a
microphone. Last Thursday started out like any other

day, she said, telling her boy to do his chores, trying not to be late for work, missing a call from him on her phone, and by the end of it, finding herself in a hospital emergency room, realizing by how people were treating her that her son must be dead.

At seventeen, she told us, she had walked across the stage at her own graduation pregnant with her boy. They grew up together. He had quit school for a while himself, overwhelmed by deaths among his peers and the general negativity about his future, but he went back and would have graduated this June. The two of them planned to go together to community college. Lord, are you serious? she said. All these years I fought for my son? All the times I told him stay off these streets? All these people who loved him? My neighbor and I were the only two white people at this gathering, but when tears started pouring down my face, a tall young man put his arm around me.

A few months later, the boy's mother attended his graduation, where he was awarded an honorary diploma. According to the *Baltimore Sun*, he was the fourth of five students from his high school to be killed during this school year. Look beyond the boundaries of Baltimore, one of the teachers urged the graduates. Their mothers must be thinking, where?

His Brother

THERE'S JUST ONE DEGREE of separation between me and Freddie Gray, who was called "Pepper" and sometimes "Freddie Black" by his friends. So I heard from one of my memoir students who knew him slightly—their connection was a hood-hopper named Gorgeous. A hood-hopper, you know, a clown who claims to be from every block in town. Anything I know about hood-hopping, or about the life of black boys in Baltimore, comes through this young writer, now the author of several published books. His career took off the week of the uprising in 2015, when he published an op-ed in the *New York Times* explaining that being beaten up by cops, as Freddie Gray was on the day of his death, was a routine part of his childhood. During basketball games. Walking to school. Anytime.

This boy was mostly raised by his older brother, a powerful and popular drug dealer who was fiercely protective of his younger sibling. He'd moved him out of their father's house when the younger boy was fifteen, desperate to keep him off the streets and in school. He hadn't finished himself, but he was a passionate reader. Their house was full of books. And basketballs, and boxes of sneakers. Three years later, the slam dunk: little brother accepted to Georgetown University! The future college student took the letter over to his mother's place to celebrate. Left a message for his big brother. Then there was a knock on the door. A breathless messenger. He ran downstairs, pushed his way through the crowd on the sidewalk.

The first thing he saw were his brother's Charles Barkleys. Still perfect, still gleaming white. His legs went limp; he flung himself onto the body. Moments later, the police arrived. They dragged him away, cuffed him, threw him in the squad car, questioned him for hours. Grief counseling, East Baltimore style.

Seventeen years later, the Baltimore police killed a man named Freddie Gray. I often wonder what Pepper would think if he could see who he has become, the strange destiny he was posthumously chosen for. His death was senseless, and it could have been meaningless, but instead it is history. So, by way of my student and his brother, by way of Gorgeous the hood-hopper, I send something I can only call a prayer.

The Grandmother-General
died 2013

THE VERY DAY WE moved to Baltimore, my nine-year-old daughter met the girl across the street, and the two have been an item ever since. These days they are big girls, playing big-girl games; I think they will be friends for life. Back when we all met, the little neighbor came with a pack of siblings, and also a rather impressive grandmother. She was a tall woman, with a lot of pepper remaining in her salt-and-pepper hair, and hastily applied but never omitted fuchsia lipstick. She had a gruff, impatient manner, and strict rules for the children, whom she shepherded every day in summer to the neighborhood pool. Sometimes I would sit with her on the bench outside the gate and smoke a cigarette. We usually discussed the novel her book club was reading; she had been in that book club for forty years. Often as we sat there, a small person would approach to report an infraction or that someone had gone missing. General Patton swung into action. Having raised six children of her own, she was a believer in the decisive response and the stiff penalty.

After putting up the fight you would expect from such a woman, she died of cancer at eighty-one. That summer, her leaderless troop drooped around the pool. It was not until I read her obituary in the *Baltimore Sun* that I really knew whom I'd been sitting next to on that bench. After graduating from college in the fifties, it said, she had hitchhiked around the U.S. and Europe, then went to work as a reporter in Connecticut. There she fell in love with another reporter; they spent the early years of their marriage running a printing press in Woodstock, New York, then moved to Baltimore so he could take a job at Hopkins. A staunch progressive, always volunteering for the Democratic Party, for local schools and liberal causes, she was deeply drawn to rural life and frugal values. So after the kids were out of the house, she and her husband bought a country store in New Hampshire. In her third act, or maybe her fifth, after he died, she came back to Baltimore to help with her grandchildren. She took in boarders, rejoined her book club, tended a garden.

Now I picture myself, blathering on about Jeffrey Eugenides or Ann Patchett, thinking I'm the one with something interesting to say.

The Role Model

died 2013

I was standing on the corner, suitcase in my hand.

I hitchhiked my way across the USA.

I put the spike into my vein.

And then things weren't quite the same.

To me, his songs were pure inspiration. In one early study of this gospel, my boyfriend and I made a 16mm black-and-white film with "Take a Walk on the Wild Side" as the soundtrack. It featured a tennis match where the main character turns from a man to a woman with each volley. I hand-colored the ball yellow in every frame; when you ran the film, it wobbled and jumped as if possessed by the devil. The point was obvious. Just as easily as a man can become a woman, a ball can become a grapefruit. And in the eighties, my friends and I would sing along to "Heroin" as we cleaned our shared syringe with a little water and passed it around.

I was standing in the lobby at some writers' event in 1997 when I heard of Allen Ginsberg's death from hepatitis. By then, I'd known I'd had the virus for about three years. It was a number on a lab report to me, nothing more. But if Ginsberg's death didn't puncture my sense of immortality, I did begin to understand something important, how big ideas about art and revolution were so easily infected with the stupid romance of self-destruction. In 2011, I suddenly got very sick, so weak I couldn't get off the couch to drive my daughter to school. In 2012, I took the cure. Not the easy, quick thing we have now, but it worked. And while I got better, Lou Reed died, as did Gregg Allman and David Bowie, as had Ken Kesey and Jim Carroll years before. Keith Richards, Steven Tyler, and I live on.

After his death, his wife, Laurie Anderson, published an article about him in *Rolling Stone*. *How strange, exciting, and miraculous*, she wrote, *that we can change each other so much, love each other so much through our words and music and our real lives.* Yes, I thought. What a beautiful couple they were. Too bad some of us were so determined to get the wrong idea.

Every band should have a cover of "Sweet Jane." This is mine.

The Talent

died 2015

Dear Ella, Leslie died last night, after a sudden, sad decline, which began about a week ago when I was cleaning her bowl and she jumped out of the strainer. How I wish I had been more careful! She injured her fin, and I think it got infected. Over the next few days she bloated up, her sleek golden body covered with an ugly red rash. When we got home from dinner last night, we found her floating upside down, stock-still and drained of color. Yet as soon as she saw me, she tried to pull herself up and wave.

The goldfish Leslie Knope began life as Pretzel and had already been through an unsuccessful adoption when a college-bound neighbor left her in our care. We changed her name and her presumptive gender, bought her an Eiffel Tower, and came to realize what a very special fish she was. As soon as she spied a visitor approaching her bowl, she would swim up, stand on her tail, and do a charming little cancan, her diaphanous, peach-colored caudal and dorsal fins sashaying as she twisted from side to side, fixing her guest with a frank and friendly gaze. She never seemed to tire of this routine, nor did I.

When I learned that under the right conditions, a goldfish can live up to fifty years, I had visions of carting her with me into assisted living. I knew that little bowl was terrible for her, and I was planning to move her into a proper tank, with a water filter and a special light, when unbelievably, accidentally, I killed her. There is no other way to say this. I could tell that night would be the end; I held the bowl in my arms and murmured soothingly. Twice I thought she was gone and took her out, only to have her wriggle back to life in my hand. I had to turn off the lights and go up to bed before she would let herself go. What a shame. But what a fish!

The French Horn Player

PERHAPS YOU DON'T THINK of Baltimore as a world capital of classical music, but it is home to a fine symphony and many smaller ensembles and orchestras, fed by a conservatory of some renown. For 150 years, the Peabody Institute has drawn young musicians to a city they've barely heard of, which turns out to be an easy place to stick around. This is how two curly-headed brothers, French horn players from South Carolina, ended up here, sharing an apartment with a view of the skateboard park. The younger one, a radiant free spirit, became friends with my son, and their love of music was not the only thing they had in common. Both were little brothers, but my son was one year older, so he considered himself the big brother in this pair. He took the young French horn player under his wing. Many long nights turned to dawn as they rocked on the porch of the apartment, like old farmers with tall tales and big schemes.

Then the boy got sick, a nasty throat infection that led to the removal of his tonsils. These days, a tonsillectomy is an outpatient procedure, forty-five minutes under anesthesia, a few hours for observation, then off you go with your antibiotics and pain medication. I was surprised to hear this, having spent days in the hospital eating lime Jell-O back in 1965, and I will not be able to tell you what happened next because all we know is that when the older brother got home from work, the boy lay dead in his room. How can that be? Every person who loved this boy, among them my son, wondered why they hadn't been with him that day. It would have been so easy. It would have been their pleasure.

The boy was buried in the foothills of Mount Catoctin, in Frederick, Maryland. A quartet of young French horn players in their concert suits performed Mahler's requiem, then his brother played an arrangement of "You Are My Sunshine" on a single horn. The notes leapt into the sky. The sun, that oldest patron of the arts, came out from behind the clouds to hear.

The Big Man

died 2016

DESTINY LOVES TO PLAY games. Like making my son's unhappy and very short-lived employment at Guitar Center the secret doorway to the future. One afternoon, a shy giant appears in the store, six foot ten in his Phillies cap, to trade in some microphones. My son races out of hiding to nab this customer—and abracadabra, our lives are changed. He entered our world like an undiscovered planet, pulling my son, his band, his friends, his mother, into his orbit. *My hands are so high, my hands are so big, just hand me that mic, I'll rock this whole crib.* A rapper is both a memoirist and a poet: I didn't get it until then, but fifteen-year-old boys all over the world were already annotating the lyrics pages on the Internet.

He had a titanic work ethic and an Olympic play ethic, he was an artistic madman with a medicine chest from hell, he had a broken biological clock that ran on breakfast sandwiches from the gas station. He had rhymes for days and stories for weeks and charms against despair: the reset button, the gray scale, the two-tone rebel, the mysterious black paisley. *Mr. Sunshine, Mr. Rainstorm, meet me in the conference room, we got to brainstorm.* After he was dead, I asked my son if he understood these metaphors. He was quiet a moment, thinking. Then we opened some beers.

Right before he went to the emergency room to see what was up, he posted a picture of his swollen hand on Twitter. That turned out to be goodbye. Like a giant in a fairy tale, he was felled by the tiniest of foes, a microorganism, a rogue in the bloodstream. We sent flowers but only his parents and sisters, tumbling through space like lost astronauts, ever saw them. *Still a Wallace in the afterlife. Music lives on, never gone, no half-life.* Why are so many of the songs about this? Even his beloved golden mutt—part retriever, part greyhound, part muse—listens to his voice over and over, wanting to believe.

The Assistant Superintendent
died 2012

MY BOSS AT THE university is a woman about my age, a slender, ukulele-playing poet with curly blond hair, a woman who governs with an unusual combination of whimsy and steel. When we met ten years ago, we both still had mothers walking the earth, and when she told me her mother had lung cancer, my mother was four years gone the same way. She had hesitated to tell me and she was right: I burst into tears. Not because our mothers were so alike, but because they were our mothers, and they were gone. Gradually, then suddenly, then completely.

A few years after her mother's death, my boss came out of her office to receive a young woman who had an appointment to discuss our program. Then stopped in her tracks. Her visitor looked as if she were already very disappointed about something, and the little girl she'd brought along seemed no happier. My boss continued straight down the hall to the ladies' room to collect herself. When she looked in the wide mirror over the sinks, her mother was there. If you have lost a parent, you probably know: that physical sense of their presence, not as a separate entity or a ghost, but as a sort of layer under your own skin. In your facial muscles, or your shoulders, or your hands. Something you would never imagine in the anguished days of your early grief; such a comfort as time goes on.

My boss's mother had worked all her life in the Baltimore schools, first teaching kindergarten and first grade and later, after earning a PhD in her spare time, as a champion of early childhood education. Before she was done, kindergarten—the true basis of social justice!—was mandatory in Baltimore. Another part of her job was to meet with various disgruntled people: parents, principals, teachers, all taken aback to see the lady with the big smile coming down the hall in her bright red suit, so happy to meet them and hear their concerns.

And so my boss left the bathroom that day, accompanied by her mother. They made a beeline for the visitors. What did she say to them? She doesn't even know. Sometimes, you just have to let them take over.

The Very Tiny Baby

died 2010

I JUST WISH THIS week could be erased from the calendar, says my cousin on the phone. It has been eight years since her baby was born too early. She weighed two pounds, lived two months, had an infection, a blood clot, and a stroke, then was gone.

When a woman loses a baby, it can go different ways. Some hold it close, keep that empty space warm forever. Others push it far away and fill the hole in their hearts with other things. I am in the second group, but my cousin is in the first. Not a day goes by, she tells me. Not a day.

My cousin looks like a girl in a Rembrandt painting with her alabaster skin and pink cheeks and corkscrew blond tresses. She has had more than her share of drastic diagnoses: dyslexia, diabetes, disability, digestive diseases. Schedules and regimes and rules that are hard to follow; a big mess when they are not.

When she turned up pregnant at twenty-four, every-one agreed she should not keep it. Everyone but her.

She made it thirty-two weeks before things started to go wrong, and she ended up on the operating table with an emergency C-section to save her own life. Her baby was whisked off to the NICU, the only home she ever had. No one can possibly imagine how hard it is to unplug the machines that are keeping your daughter alive, even if she is the size of a Coke can and they tell you she is brain-dead.

Tomorrow's her birthday, says my cousin. She would be eight. We go to the cemetery every year.

His Dog

ONCE UPON A TIME there was a woman who wanted a dog, but her husband said no. A dog is too much trouble. We have enough to worry about. Then some friends had triplets and someone had to take their black Lab. The Lab, it turned out, was an impeccably trained dog who never needed a leash, never barked or whined, let little girls put their hands in her mouth and ride around on her back. But as well trained as she was, the Lab would occasionally run away overnight, and the man would suffer unbearable anxiety. So when the woman wanted to get a second dog, he said definitely not.

Then his brother gave them a puppy for Hanukkah, an eight-week-old ball of white fluff with pink bows on her ears. Immediately she started following the big dog around, chasing her long black tail. One wag would send her flying across the room. Then she'd come back for more. Who says no to that?

The years went by. The big dog died, the daughters grew up and went away, and the woman was busy, too. She was never as crazy about the miniature poodle as she had been about the Lab, and the husband, who was an emotional guy, felt the dog was a little bit lost. He started taking her with him into his studio all day. She became his assistant director, his sous-chef, his sidekick. Some people may have thought he was obsessed with the dog. As she got older and increasingly fragile, he worried about her more and more. Then, at thirteen, she developed a serious heart condition and had to wear diapers. The wife said it was time to put her down. But he just couldn't.

When they left for Europe the wife said, Say goodbye. He tried. Then he got the text from the house sitter as soon as they got off the plane in Amsterdam. He called me from the airport. What do I do now, he said, and he started to cry.

This is why he didn't want a dog.

The Pirate

dead to me, 2017

AFTER MY DIVORCE, I got disillusioned with the dating sites and went on Craigslist, where I found an intriguing post with a photo of a recently divorced, good-looking guy running on a beach. One hundred and thirty-eight emails later, I drove to Annapolis to meet this man, who lived on a sailboat. That day, after a long, adolescent kiss on a park bench, I became obsessed with him. Unfortunately, this caused him to flee from me entirely.

I forgot all about it, except I didn't. Every October 3, the anniversary of the kiss, I would think of him, and some years I would write and say hi. In 2016, he suggested we meet again, and we returned to Annapolis, where we made out in a parking garage. This time he was very clear that he was not looking for a relationship. Neither was I, at least not with him, because now I had enough distance to realize what a player he was. I didn't care. In this stage of my life I was much less motivated by desire than in my younger years, but somehow this particular bug bite was still very itchy.

Eventually plans were made for an indoor meeting. They fell apart repeatedly, but I bided my time. One morning in early December, three minutes after my daughter had left for school, he showed up at my door. One thousand butterflies flew all through the house. And I have never seen him again, though appointments were made and cancelled. Then he mentioned that he was involved with someone else. I bid him adieu.

In September 2017, I received the first phone call I ever got from him. My wife would like to speak to you, he said. Then a woman got on the phone—his second wife, I would imagine, though I'm not completely sure where she fits in the timeline—who had just read 573 emails between her husband and me. She said she just wanted to tell me that he had herpes, but he probably got it from his other girlfriend. Yes, she shouted, there's another one. He's cheating on you, too! I had a few things I wanted to say, like I didn't know he was married and I'm sorry, but before I could open my mouth, she hung up. I wasn't all that sorry, anyway.

He probably isn't dead, but if he is, I hope she has a good lawyer.

The Happy Man

.... died 2017 ....

YEARS AGO, A STUDENT in my journalism class chose an interesting Baltimorean for her profile assignment. A guy whose passion for social justice had led him through career number one, criminal law, to career number two, public health, to career number three, Importer of Magnificent Treasures and Patron Saint of Nepalese Villages, to career number four, dress designer. On a soul-searching global sabbatical in his early forties, he'd had a vision: a store that would sell crafts produced by third-world people, funneling its profits back to their villages to fund schools. By the mid-1990s, he'd made that happen; even more successfully, he developed a line of women's clothing made from handmade textiles. His shop in downtown Baltimore had a reputation not just for fine merchandise but also for uncanny powers of mood enhancement. Half the time people come in here just to cheer up, one of the employees told my cub reporter.

Years later, after I moved to Baltimore, I met a pair of twins at my daughter's elementary school, then realized this man was their father. I saw him most often in summer at our neighborhood pool, tall and lean, with dark curly hair and a great, lopsided nose, swimming what seemed like hundreds of laps each morning. For some reason, my social anxiety is at its worst at the pool, where I make a beeline to a chair, stick my head in my book, and never speak to anyone. He was the only person not put off by my wall of bad vibes, stopping each day to say hello. He had a joyous smile that involved his whole face, his warm brown eyes and thick brows seeming to acknowledge that there are many reasons not to smile and we know that, but let's smile anyway.

He was seventy but looked fifty when he died in a motorcycle accident in Nepal, a bad one in the middle of nowhere or his remarkable vigor might have pulled him through. According to the slide show we watched at his memorial, the man simply could not be caught without a smile on his face, from his bar mitzvah in Brooklyn on out. And as brokenhearted as his mourners may have been, no one could speak of him without giving in to the urge, even his wife. Think of what he would want to happen, she said, and see that it does.

The Babydaddy

I HEARD THE STORY of The Babydaddy before I met him, from the mother of one of my fourth-grade daughter's friends. She had briefly dated a man twenty years older than she; they broke up because he already had a bunch of troubled kids and an expensive ex-wife, while she had a ticking clock. Shortly after she met someone new, she learned she was pregnant with the older man's child. Surprisingly, her new suitor urged her to keep the baby and volunteered to raise it with her. This was the guy I knew as the little girl's father. While The Babydaddy had been tetchy about the plan at first—new support payments just as he was beginning his retirement—he ended up quite in love with the last addition to his family. They spent every Sunday together for many years.

In eighth grade, the girls went on a trip with their Spanish teacher to Peru and parents were allowed to join. This was when I finally met him, a quiet, mostly good-natured graybeard with hair combed back from a widow's peak, a man of moderate views and conservative habits. Then I learned he actually had two daughters on this trip, the other a packet of cremains in his suitcase. His eldest, dead in her forties of an overdose. Half of her went into the Pacific at Lima, and the other half almost didn't make it to Machu Picchu, as heavy rains kept us in town for an extra day. Then the gods relented.

His tall silhouette and his daughter's small one, hiking up to the Temple of the Sun.

That was the last I heard of him until the girls' senior year of high school, when I got a call asking for photos that might be used at his memorial. At seventy-two, he had collapsed on a staircase, already dead when he reached the bottom. He didn't drink, he hadn't been ill—in fact, in his sixties, he'd become a gym rat, convening daily in the sauna with his retired cronies. I found two pictures of him in Peru. One bravely trying the local fermented corn drink, the other opposite his daughter at a long table in a restaurant. She in an orange beanie, looking wide-eyed at the camera, and he in profile, smiling straight at her.

The Innocents

died 1966, 1999, 2007, 2012, 2018 . . .

IN THE CURRENT ISSUE of *People* magazine, it is sand-
wiched between "What Went Wrong Between Jennifer Aniston and Justin Theroux" and "Amy Schumer's
Surprise Wedding." A two-page spread of a candle-
light vigil, followed by the now-familiar story. The
fire drill at the end of the school day. The gunshots,
the text messages, the SWAT team. People doubled
over, people covering their faces, people wailing into
cell phones. *I don't know what hell is like but it can't be
worse than what I saw at that school.* The roll call of the
dead, their glowing faces and miniature biographies: a
sports career, a college scholarship, a love of the beach,
a smile as bright as a firecracker. I don't blame *People*
magazine for this. It is the news, it is what happens,
right in the middle of everything.

More often than not it is one of my children who
first tells me there has been a mass shooting. Mom,
I think something terrible happened in Colorado.

In Virginia. In Las Vegas. In Florida. At the country music festival, the elementary school, the college campus, the nightclub, the church. The Amish schoolhouse. The Jewish community center. The mosque. The movie theater. The high school.

It's the image of children crossing a parking lot as if in a conga line, hands on shoulders, wearing the colorful jackets and bright, clean sneakers their mothers sent them to school in, that haunts me. Just as kids used to practice what to do in case of fire or nuclear attack, they now learn the correct procedures in case of mass murder. Get under the desk. Get in the closet. Stay away from the windows. Run. Our president has a suggestion: more guns. More yellow tape, more candles, more flowers. Teddy bear stock is on the rise.

To be a parent is to have your heart go walking around outside your body, as the writer Elizabeth Stone put it. At every moment, it is exactly as terrifying as you can tolerate. There is so much you have to turn away from just to get through a day. Now the eerie conga line files through our dreams. The phone rings. This is too much to ask of us.

The Leader of the Pack

died 2012

GOOD MORNING, LADIES OF the dog world! my neighbor would trill at 5 a.m. Since she was just on the other side of the wall in the duplex we share, it was a good thing that this was the very hour my eyes popped open of their own accord. My neighbor, a soft-edged blonde no older than I, lived alone with two dogs and a cat. Sally, being part border collie, was a bit smarter than her younger companion Kayley, a shepherd mutt. Chase the Cat had moved in from a few doors down.

After that morning greeting, my neighbor would address a running commentary to her pets throughout the day, usually on topics of mutual interest, such as the weather, the plans for a walk, or the prohibition against eating poo. I say this not in judgment but as a woman who is more or less married to a thirteen-year-old miniature dachshund, a mostly deaf dog called by a dozen different silly names and serenaded daily with customized theme songs.

Sally had a long decline, but after she could no longer stand, my neighbor called the mobile vet to come with her syringe. Kayley and Chase went to her son's house during the procedure; when they returned, Sally's body had been stowed in the back of the RAV4 until the opening of the crematorium at the SPCA. I learned all this when I came outside and found my neighbor gently leading Kayley to the car to view the body. After the dog had said her goodbyes, my neighbor took her inside and came out carrying Chase the Cat. I'm giving them closure, she explained.

At the time, I thought this was over the top, but having just read a book on animal grief—the mourning of sea turtles, dolphins, rabbits, and horses—I learned she did just the right thing. Luckily, Kayley and Chase still had each other, and neither went on to exhibit the classic symptoms of bereavement: loss of appetite, lethargy, unusual howling or yowling, pacing or keeping vigil. By the time Kayley died three years later, my neighbor had begun to pad her pack. I think there might be three or four cats over there now. With my daughter leaving for college next fall, I've followed her lead, taking in a young puss to keep me and the dachshund company. Good morning, lovey pets, good morning!

El Suegro

died 2017

THOUGH MY OLDER SON met the Ecuadoran girl who is now his wife back when they were in college, and has known her parents almost as long, I did not meet her father until just before the wedding.

I first saw his picture the day of the engagement, which was an elaborate scavenger hunt all over Boston, at the end of which my son's ladylove found him kneeling in the street with a ring. Her mother and I had flown in to take part in this extravaganza, but her father couldn't make it. He had been formally asked for her hand, and had given his blessing.

My son is very reserved about the fact that his own father died when he was six, which is kind of funny given all my published work on the subject, or perhaps makes perfect sense. It explains why my son's mother-in-law-to-be saw a picture of Tony for the first time at the engagement party. She looked at me wide-eyed and found an old photo of her husband in her phone. When they were in their thirties, they could have been brothers.

This resemblance seemed magical to me, especially knowing how much my son admired this man. He was a financier—my son's field—and a perfect gentleman, a modest introvert who never talked about himself, with a unusual combination of South American Catholic traditionalism and intellectual openness. My son only learned much later the glamorous story of his career before the national financial crisis that inspired the family's move to the United States.

Immediately after the engagement, he was diagnosed with pancreatic cancer. He tried so hard to beat it, it almost seemed he might. It was a feat of pure will that the wedding went off as planned. That day, you might not even have known he was ill, so replete was he with the joy of the occasion that he almost filled out his tailored suit. In his welcoming toast, he spoke warmly of my son. For one short moment, I felt like fate was trying to make it up to us.

After his father's death, my son developed a phobia of hospitals, but in the last days of El Suegro, he was

there all the time. I loved picturing him in the bab-
bling cluster of Spanish speakers at the bedside. And
I love seeing him in the fine wool coat he inherited,
too, though it breaks my heart.

The Living

MY GOOD FRIEND HAS a last name everyone in Baltimore knows: the same as a historic neighborhood and its main thoroughfare. In 1839, his great-great-grandfather was one of the investors in the city's first public cemetery—Green Mount, a classic name for a classic burial ground in the Victorian "rural garden" style. When you drive though the brick arch of the Gothic guardhouse, you could be traveling through time as well as space, from a rundown urban block in the twenty-first century to a misty moor in times gone by.

It could have been Jared Leto playing the bearded watchman. He put down the book he was reading—E. M. Cioran—to sign us in and give us a map. Down Oliver's Walk, we found the spot where my friend and his husband will someday lie. Beside his mother and father, near generals, mayors, and governors, among happy and unhappy wives and pioneer lesbians. On the back of my friend's mother's tombstone she requested a list of all ten of her children's names. As much as any Civil War battle, an achievement of note.

In winter, Green Mount offers a panorama of quietly graying neighborhoods, splashed here and there with bright-colored murals and graffiti. In warmer months, the sycamore, locust, oak, and maple fill in with leaves; cardinals and ravens arrive to build their nests. Occasionally birdwatchers have seen a falcon or owl, probably as surprised to find this little utopia as I was. According to the philosopher-watchman, there are seventy-seven thousand dead at Green Mount; new arrivals are down to about ten per year. One day my friend will be among them, joining his ancestors in the earth of their shared hometown, his love at his side.

For me, there is a lidded ceramic vase waiting on a small table in the corner of my living room, tucked behind two similar urns and an ice bucket. The urns contain the ashes of my first husband and our still-born son. My mother was supposed to have the third, but while it was on order, she was temporarily stored in the silver ice bucket she and my father won for the 1965 Husband and Wife tournament at Hollywood Golf Club, and actually, that was just right. My father's ashes were stolen from the back of a jewelry drawer by a misguided robber in the 1990s.

As my friend said that day at Green Mount, I don't mind the thought of joining them. But no time soon.

Notes

The Brother-in-Law: You can read more about his family in The Skater and The Quiet Guy in *The Glen Rock Book of the Dead*.

Who Dat: I originally described the assisted suicide in an August 1994 commentary for *All Things Considered*; this grew into a section of *First Comes Love*. There is an essay devoted to the topic, "My New Neighborhood," in *Above Us Only Sky*.

The Artist: Steve is remembered as The Carpenter in *The Glen Rock Book of the Dead*.

The Young Hercules and The Neatnik: The software company mentioned in these two is also the setting of The Democrat and The Wunderkind in *The Glen Rock Book of the Dead*. The Democrat was the boss's mother, also the Young Hercules's grandmother.

The Queen of the Scene: The quote is from "She's About a Mover," by Margaret Moser, which appeared in the Winter 2014 issue of the *Oxford American*.

The Paid Professional Codependent: The friend who committed suicide was The Bon Vivant in *The Glen Rock Book of the Dead*.

The Southern Writer: The book is *Wolf Whistle*, by Lewis Nordan. The comparison to the blues was originally made by Michael Harris, in a review in the *Los Angeles Times*.

The Rancher: Her sons are remembered in The Texan in *The Glen Rock Book of the Dead*.

The Old Rake: The third wife mentioned here is The Realtor from *The Glen Rock Book of the Dead*, and that was the same trip to Venice. The lines quoted are Gary Cartwright's, from *Texas Monthly*.

The Belligerent Stream: I learned about the burial of the Jones Falls from a coffee-table book called *Lost Baltimore*, by Gregory J. Alexander and Paul Kelsey Williams, and read more about it in Sergey Kadinsky's *Hidden Waters Blog*, hiddenwatersblog .wordpress.com. The secret waterfall appeared in *Kill Me Now*, by Timmy Reed.

The Very Tiny Baby: My own stillborn son is the subject of The Baby in *The Glen Rock Book of the Dead.*

The Leader of the Pack: The book I mention is *How Animals Grieve*, by Barbara J. King.

Acknowledgments

For every piece in this book, there is at least one person who got a phone call, email, or Facebook message from me out of the blue, asking for help. Thank you so much, Joyce Abell, Amy Abramson, Patricia Albright, Maria Baquerizo, Lori Beveridge, Sarah Bird, Jessica Anya Blau, Steve Bolton, Cindy Bonner, Dorothy Browne, Kathy Caruso, Victoria Caruso, Kay Curry, Carolyn Dryden, Ellen Ducote, Laura Emberson, Judy Frels, Mary Friedman, Sarah Gleason, Meredith Jones Gonzalez, Sandy Goolsby, Liz Hazen, Debbie Heubach, Dallas Hlatky, Morgan Jones, Jeff Joslin, Cathy Kapschull, Nancy Kirkwood, Kendra Kopelke, Kathy Korniloff, Pete LaBonne, Liz Lambert, James Magruder, Kim McGowan, Jane Metzendorf, Naomi Shihab Nye, the Payne family, Doug Preston, Jan Ralske, Timmy Reed, Sandye Renz, Dubravka Romano, Kristen Romano, Jane Sartwell, Nancy Seeback, Jessica Shahin, J.C. Stamler, Pam Stein, Ava Taylor, Havely Taylor, Scott Van Osdol, D Watkins, Robin

Whitney, Hayes Winik, Vince Winik, Holly Winter, and Carla Work. Thank you, Jack Shoemaker, for saying yes, and thank you, Jennifer Alton, Megan Fishmann, Wah-Ming Chang, Barrett Briske, and Katie Boland, for your help and enthusiasm. For the beautiful cover image, my admiration and gratitude to Andrew B. Myers, Jenny Carrow, and art director Nicole Caputo. Thanks also to my darlings, Beau and Squash, always by my side.

Author photograph by Maeve Secor & Jane Sartwell

Longtime *All Things Considered* commentator MARION WINIK is the author of *First Comes Love*, *The Glen Rock Book of the Dead*, and seven other books. Her Bohemian Rhapsody column at BaltimoreFishbowl.com has received the Best Column and Best Humorist awards from *Baltimore* magazine, and her essays have been published in *The New York Times Magazine*, *The Sun*, and many other publications. She is the host of *The Weekly Reader* radio show and podcast, based at the Baltimore NPR affiliate. She reviews books for *Newsday*, *People*, and *Kirkus Reviews* and is a board member of the National Book Critics Circle. She is a professor in the MFA program at the University of Baltimore. Find more at marionwinik.com.